THE TERROR OF
❋ HISTORY ❋

THE TERROR OF
HISTORY

ON THE UNCERTAINTIES OF LIFE
IN WESTERN CIVILIZATION

TEOFILO F. RUIZ

PRINCETON UNIVERSITY PRESS

PRINCETON AND OXFORD

Published by Princeton University Press, 41 William Street,
Princeton, New Jersey 08540
In the United Kingdom: Princeton University Press, 6 Oxford Street,
Woodstock, Oxfordshire OX20 1TW

press.princeton.edu

Library of Congress Cataloging-in-Publication Data
Ruiz, Teofilo F., 1943–
The terror of history : on the uncertainties of life in Western civilization /
Teofilo F. Ruiz.
p.   cm.
Includes bibliographical references and index.
ISBN 978-0-691-12413-1 (hardcover : acid-free paper) 1. Civilization, Western.
2. Uncertainty—Social aspects—History. 3. Terror—Social aspects—History.
4. Disasters—Social aspects—History. 5. Adjustment (Psychology)—History.
I. Title.
CB251.R85 2011
909′.09821—dc22   2011011127

British Library Cataloging-in-Publication Data is available

This book has been composed in Minion

Printed on acid-free paper. ∞

Printed in the United States of America

1 3 5 7 9 10 8 6 4 2

To My Students

CONTENTS

PREFACE

IN EARLY FALL 2005 with throngs of tourists still in oppressive display and warmed by a shimmering Tuscan sun, I meandered through the streets of Florence, seeking, in the Oltrarno piazza di Santo Spirito, some relief from the crowds. Thinking already of this book, I tried to imagine what it would have been like to walk through the city in 1348. Though reliving the past is not always advisable or even desirable, to a present-day visitor 1348 Florence would have been both uncannily familiar and unfamiliar. For one, the smells, noise, and activity of a medieval city, especially one as large as Florence which had around 100,000 inhabitants early that year, would have shaken the modern sensibilities of most Westerners. Yet, the significant landmarks that twentieth-first-century tourists seek so devoutly and in such appalling numbers—the Duomo, the Palazzo Vecchio, the piazza de la Signoria, the Ponte Vecchio, or the Franciscan church of Santa Croce—already dominated the city's landscape in the mid-fourteenth century. Nothing however would have prepared the modern traveler for the horror that beset Florence and other parts of Europe later that year.

Although we may know—thanks to the works of many historians that provide comprehensive accounts of the Black Death and its impact—far better than Florentines did in 1348 all the social, economic, cultural, and demographic consequences of the plague, we have unwittingly reduced the historicizing of these events to mere scholarship. In doing so, we have robbed the plague of its cruel immediacy and reality as a felt experience in time. So allow me to retell to you one of the grimmest stories in the long and troubled history of the West and the world. Late in 1348 few would have walked the city in admiration of its new and beautiful civic and religious landmarks. That year, as was the case in most parts of Europe, a violent and often deadly form of pestilence struck the city. It delivered an almost fatal blow to Florentine and European societies, to their morale, to their sensibilities. Perhaps as much as half the population of the city died within a short period of time. The poor, as was the case in the tragedy unleashed by Hurricane Katrina in 2005, died in greater proportion than other segments of the population. So did the Jews, in spite of much repeated and mistaken assertions to the contrary. Parents abandoned their children and vice versa, husbands their wives. Selfless behavior and piety were often rewarded by horrible death. Selfishness, often articulated by fleeing the ill or ceasing all contact with the sick, gave a fleeting hope of survival. All around Europe, the experiences were more or less the same. For a period of almost six months— usually the time it took the sickness to vanquish those most vulnerable—life came to a stop. Governments, ecclesiastical institutions, and individuals proved incapable of dealing with the onslaught of the Black Death.

Pestilence, originating in the East, had made its way slowly along trade routes until it reached the shores of the Aegean Sea, and, then, carried by ship, Sicily. Shortly afterwards it entered the Italian peninsula and spread to other parts of Europe. Transmitted by fleabites or through airborne contamination (delivered through sneezing or coughing), death from bubonic pestilence was particularly painful and graphic. Boils in the armpits, groin, or neck, and livid marks on the body (from which the description of the sickness as the "Black Death" derives) were followed by internal hemorrhage, uncontrolled diarrhea, the spitting of blood, and other such horrific symptoms. Fortunately for the suffering victims and relatives, the end was swift. In modern Western society, where we hide our sick and dying in hospitals or similar institutions, we cannot even begin to comprehend the impact of such illness even to a society, such as that of the Middle Ages, where squalor, poverty, and disease were part of the quotidian patterns of life. Florence's experiences were replicated in other towns and villages throughout the West, eliciting reflections from witnesses who experienced the Black Death close at hand. Agnolo di Tura, known as "the Fat" and a citizen of Siena, tells us that he buried his children with his own hands, one of those cases in which a father did not flee the illness of his children but remained behind to care for and bury them. Monasteries, providing the ideal setting for transmission, were decimated. In some places, as for example northern Castile, documentary evidence seems to stop for almost a decade after the plague, as if life and the memorializing of death, transfers of property, and other activities that form the pattern of people's lives had all come to an unwanted stop. Among those recording the tragedy, no one did so with more chilling accuracy than Giovanni Boccaccio, noted writer, member of the Church, citizen of Florence, and witness to the plague in his beloved city. In the preface to his enchanting *Decameron*, Boccaccio provides us with a road map to the debilitating sickness and, more importantly, to the manner in which the citizens of Florence reacted to its onslaught.

In seeking to explain the causes of the Black Death and its trajectory through Florence, Boccaccio presents his readers with a host of possible explanations. It came, he tells us, either "because of the influence of heavenly bodies or because of God's just wrath as a punishment to mortals for our wicked deeds...."[1] As Boccaccio describes it, in the face of the plague's assault, people responded in a variety of ways. Pious supplications and religious processions were of no avail. Some withdrew from the sick and lived a life of moderation, eating and drinking only the finest foods and drinks, speaking not of death. Others embraced life by engaging in constant revelry, debauchery, and drunkenness. A few chose the middle course, going out into the world with flowers close to their nostrils to avoid the miasma, with posies in their pockets, as the nursery rhyme tells us, before "we all fall down." Others fled into the countryside in search of safety. And yet others, as Boccaccio did, sought to escape or to make meaning of the catastrophe by writing. Nothing helped. For death pursued those who stayed and those who fled equally, slaying them randomly.

In Boccaccio's introduction to his delightfully wicked and obscene collection of stories, the *Decameron*, we have clear guideposts as to the manner in which humans tend to react to great catastrophes. We can shorten them to three or four specific categories, to be explored in greater detail in the next chapter. First and foremost humans embraced religion to explain and to find some solace from the overwhelming brutality of the plague. Religion in Boccaccio's time served two specific and inherently contradictory purposes. One, it contained the hope of stopping, reversing, or delaying the catastrophe itself. That is, in Boccaccio's Florence, processions aimed, first and foremost, at stopping the plague by divine intervention and by atoning for human sins and, thus, gaining for-

---

[1] Giovanni Boccaccio, *The Decameron*, trans. and ed. Mark Musa and Peter E. Bondanella (New York: Norton, 1977) 3.

giveness and the lifting of God's wrath from the shoulders of humans. At the same time, accepting God's inscrutable actions served to shift the burden of the inexplicable to the actions of the divinity. It is awful, but God, or, as I may tend to say through this book, "god" (like father) knows best.

There is a saying in Spanish, *a Dios rogando y con el mazo dando*, that is, "to god praying while hitting with the hammer at the same time," which can be roughly the equivalent of "god helps those who help themselves." So other actions, besides processions and prayers (which after all proved so ineffectual in mid-fourteenth-century Florence and elsewhere), were needed. Some embraced the material world, stating through their wanton deeds that if one was going to die, one might as well have fun doing it. Drinking, cavorting, fornicating were in some respects a carnal alternative to prayer and an admission of the hopelessness of the situation. Eating fine foods and drinking fine wines, refusing to speak of death or of ugly things is also a way of embracing the material world. And then there were those who fled. Like Boccaccio's protagonists in the *Decameron*; some left the city for the countryside, sought refuge in their country palaces, and there lived well, while telling amusing and delectable stories to each other. In some respects, the writing of the *Decameron* itself was an aesthetic response to the cruelty of the plague. Telling stories, especially salty and humorous ones, was another form of combating the darkness settling over Europe.

There is, of course, another response that historians often neglect: those who stayed, cared for the sick, went on with the grim details of everyday life. Those who buried the dead, sometimes their own children and wives, with their own hands. Those who helped others. Those who did not get drunk, engage in licentious behavior, did not write books. In writing about the ways of escaping history and facing the horrors of what I will call the "terror of history"—the wreckage of human history, the catastrophes, and the like—we often neglect to tell about those who go on in their dogged way to keep the world afloat and who seek to endure in the face of great trials. Those who are tested greatly and yet manage to continue with their lives. Having seen Spike Lee's moving documentary on the breaking of the levees in New Orleans, all the following responses found in Boccaccio's description of the plague in Florence apply equally: from those who turned to god to those who sought, even through looting, material goods and revelry, to those who fled the city in the face of the incompetence and neglect of the authorities and the federal government. What is inspiring however are the small sacrifices, the small acts of courage and defiance in the face of the inexplicable horror of the hurricane and the subsequent neglect. In the pages that follow, I will focus on these three responses—religion, embracing the material world, and the aesthetic response to tragedy—but we should not forget those who do not give in and who, through their sacrifices and constancy, keep the horror at bay, keep us from descending into utter chaos and darkness. In doing so, they give us hope.

As I begin my reflections on these issues and on the human response to the terror of history, I remember a heartfelt e-mail I received several years ago. I had done some audio and video tapes for the Teaching Company. In one of them, I defined religion, material cultural, and even aesthetic preoccupations as forms of escapes. One perceptive and thoughtful listener wrote to me passionately of her own reflection on that terrible quandary—a quandary, a question that is as old as human consciousness itself—which we all face. Even though we may deploy myriad of ways to cope with the sad realities of the world and of human history, yet we know, or many of us think we know, deep inside our guts, so my correspondent wrote, that the whole elaborate array of ways of distracting ourselves, of coping with the inexplicable, of dealing with the terrible things that life and history sometimes throw our individual and collective ways are illusions. That, intrinsically, these palliatives to the terror of history have no validity of their own; that they are nothing but a mirage. That "history," in Ruth Mackay's formulation, "is a cross we bear."[2] It is that mirage, that "cross," and what to do about this forbidden and terrible knowledge that I wish to discuss in the pages that follow.

This book, like most of my books, has been very long in the making. But it has also been an enduring source of agony. It is difficult for a professional historian to stand aside from his or her métier and write a book in which the personal continuously intrudes into the narrative. A book without notes? A book with a minimum of scholarly apparatus, in which the personal, heartfelt as it may be, and the disciplinary conventions overlap? Impossible! But here it is. And I owe, as always, many thanks to many people. First and foremost, the idea for the course on mystics, heretics, and witches that I have been teaching for so many years and that led eventually to these reflections was borrowed *in toto* from Theodore K. Rabb's magnificent graduate seminar at Princeton almost four decades ago. Over as many years, I have also benefitted from the comments, observations, and responses of thousands of students who have enrolled in and attended this particular class at Brooklyn College, Princeton University, and now UCLA. They have been the true inspiration for this book, and many of the ideas and responses discussed here

---

[2] Ruth MacKay, *"Lazy and Improvident People": Myth and Reality in the Writing of Spanish History* (Ithaca, NY: Cornell University Press, 2006) 249.

summarize numberless conversations and discussions with these inquisitive young men and women. It is their work as much as mine. I have also been very fortunate to receive many e-mails and letters from those watching my taped lectures for the Teaching Company. Although these taped lectures are very different from the contents of this book, the response and queries I have received regarding my historical discussion of these topics have led me to reflect further on the meaning of these movements and their place in history. In most of my acknowledgments to other books, I include a long list of historians and friends whose work has impacted how I think and write about historical issues. Here I will not impose on them a book that is personal rather than historical. Nonetheless, I would be remiss were I not to thank Mark Pegg for his insightful comments and support. Jesús Rodríguez Velasco provided me with the most heartfelt and thoughtful reading of this manuscript. If I have not followed his comments as much as I should, it is because only Jesús could write that book. Peter Brown, "the master of those who know," may not remember delectable lunches long ago in Trenton. I do. Our conversations there provided a great deal of the kernel for this book. His comments now have been invaluable. Paul Freedman has been a constant source of support and inspiration. My wife, friend, and fellow conspirator, Scarlett, is the reason I have not succumbed to the terror of history. At the Princeton University Press, Sarah Wolfe and Sara Lerner have been most helpful in getting this book to you. Eva Jaunzems has carefully and lovingly copyedited the book. I am most grateful for her help in dealing with my many grammatical and stylistic infelicities. Finally, Brigitta van Rheinberg believed, and continued to believe, in this book when I did not do so fully. She has been a loyal friend, a superb reader, editor, and commentator. In many respects, this book is as much hers as it is mine. The mistakes and excesses, I fear, are all mine.

Paris and Los Angeles, 2010

THE TERROR OF
❊ HISTORY ❊

❈ I ❈

THE TERROR OF HISTORY

FOR MORE THAN THREE DECADES, I have taught an under-graduate course entitled, as this book partly is, "The Terror of History." The class examines the development of mysticism, heresy, magic, and witchcraft in medieval and early modern Europe. I often have large enrollments in my classes, but none compare to the crowds that attend my lectures on these subjects. I have long thought that students flock to this particular course because of the unorthodox nature of the topics discussed, but year after year I am struck by the many students who eagerly take the class for more than its esoteric or "magical" aspects. They come—many of them do—seeking answers to existential fears, seeking to understand and deal with the harshness of the world in which they live.

One could argue that college students—often coming from well-to-do families and being impossibly young—seldom know about the angst and anxieties provoked by historical events and existential questions. In these materialistic and apathetic times in which we live, spiritual concerns are, more often than not, overshadowed by the pursuit of commodities, a career, or a good job. Law school, often chosen without any real sense of what the law is or what it is for, beats the reflected life most of the time. But to my amazement a large number of students not only take the class but also come to my office with heartfelt queries about their place in the world, articulating, as honestly as only the young can often do, their fears and uncertainties, questioning their faith or lack of it. This is even more touching since my own approach, a fairly skeptical one, posits mystical experiences and belief in witchcraft as forms of escape from history or, often, in a harsh functionalist fashion only possible in lower-division undergraduate courses, as part of the way in which those on top rule or deploy belief and persecution to advance their own agendas and power. This book is, in some respects, an honest attempt to answer those students' queries raised over the many years I have taught, and to provide some explanations that go beyond (and seek to debunk) many of the fictionalized or self-help accounts that are now popular among the reading public. Over the last two decades or so such books, from popular studies of the occult, to fictional recreations of mysteries à la Dan Brown, or self-help books, have had a hold on the popular imagination.

This book is also an attempt to answer these questions for myself, for, despite the more than three decades that I have been teaching and writing, I am still uncertain as to what the answers are, or, worse yet, if there are any answers at all. Teaching this quarter (fall term 2010), an introductory class on world history from the Big Bang to around 500 CE, reading with the students texts ranging from the *Epic of Gilgamesh,* to the *Avestas,* the *Life of the Buddha,* the *Gita,* and other such books, I have become even more confused that I have ever been, but also more keenly aware of our endless search as humans for meaning.

What Is This Book All About?

In the simplest of formulations, this book is a reflection or meditation on how men and women in Western society have sought to make meaning of the world in which they live and of the often troubling historical events that serve as the context for their individual and collective lives. This book is also about the manner in which they have managed to do this in both mundane and unusual ways, ranging from the embrace of religious experiences to the pursuit of the material world to the quest for aesthetic bliss. These actions and beliefs may seem, at times, a form of escapism, as ways in which certain individuals and groups hoped to flee from the death-grip of history and build alternative and, often, ahistorical lives. But this book also reflects on the meanings and usefulness of these diverse attempts to confront the weight of history and the uncertainty of the world.

In the chapters that follow, I examine only a few and discrete instances of the ways in which men and women have tried, and continue to try, to make sense of the world in the long period between roughly the ancient world and the recent past. My inquiry, thematic rather than chronological, ranges across the centuries, highlighting specific communal or individual patterns of behavior, with examples of how some individuals and groups in the West faced and escaped the cruelty of their times. I do not argue that these experiences were replicated in different periods, or that they are all the same. Each age provided its own unique setting, and its own responses to the crises shaped by these shifting contexts. Nor do I claim that these experiences or responses were or are universal. They were and are not. And if I ever did, teaching world history has certainly cured me of that. Moreover, if my emphasis is on the experience of Western men and women, that follows from my own expertise and knowledge of European society and my very limited understanding of other parts of the world. Nonetheless, I am certain that a similar and perhaps far more meaningful book could be written about other regions of the world.

I have long thought, pondered, and taught about these matters. I do not claim, in any case and as I wrote before, to have answers to these questions or to be able, by some clear and direct formulation, to explain the complex mechanisms that prompt human beings to react in often unpredictable fashion to historical or natural catastrophes. I am, in many respects, often as confused and clueless as my young freshmen and sophomore students are sometimes. Age, I fear, does not necessarily confer wisdom. What I do claim is an enduring desire to grapple with these issues and try to come up with as honest an answer as I can to what is one of the central themes in human history: how do we act and react in the face of terrible challenges in our lives? Why? At the core of this reflection is also a wish to see and understand history and historical processes not in a Whiggish or linear fashion but histor(ies) as unfolding, unpredictable, and contentious contexts for our lives. Far more significant, these reflections seek to understand why we often have such an inexhaustible desire to make and have meaning. Tragedy, as a literary trope but also as a form of self-representation and a form of life, is inherent in historical processes.

What Is the Terror of History?

Anxieties about the world in which we live and about our individual lives are not unique or exclusive to small groups of susceptible young students or aging cynical scholars. We all, to some degree or another, are susceptible to these pressures and seek, in myriad ways, to insulate ourselves from the stress of history. After all, personal tragedies and stresses, as well as wider historical phenomena, affect almost everyone. They range from quotidian preoccupations about family, jobs, and personal relations to the broader collective concerns of war, national policies, international strife, and ecological disasters. In today's world, we are constantly reminded of the cruelties of history by the onslaught of printed and visual news, by commentary and spinning. Any fairly reasonable human who reads the news or watches the international scene cannot but be shaken in the belief that the world is all right or even rational. The flip side to civil and ordered societies is genocide in Darfur, sectarian violence in Iraq, Palestine, Kashmir, and elsewhere, wanton and inexplicable violence on our campuses, appalling natural disasters, governmental neglect bordering on the criminal, and other such recurring events. There, in the endless strife of our world, personal and collective concerns intersect, provoking fears and anxieties that are always felt at two levels: by individuals and by members of wider communities.

These fears are not new, nor are they necessarily related to an increase in media coverage. We share them with our ancestors. We share them with prehistoric people. In a dramatic chapter entitled "The Terror of History" (from which I have shamelessly borrowed my own title), the always suggestive and engaging Mircea Eliade examines how early homo sapiens' dread of the evening, uncertainty about the sun's comforting rise every morning and the return of spring, and our own fear of an atomic holocaust—a fear most vivid when Eliade wrote his book, *Cosmos and History,* more than half a century ago—affected, and continue to affect, the way we see history and the future.

Borrowing from Eliade, I argue that the unpredictability of history—the weight of endless cycles of war, oppression, and cruelty beyond description—shapes our individual and collective lives. Few have the courage or cold existential resignation of Meursault, Camus' protagonist in *The Stranger*, or Meursault's ability to look at the blank and indifferent face of the universe and "to open [himself] for the first time to the tender indifference of the world" ("... je m'ouvrais pour la première fois à la tendre indifférence du monde"). Most of humanity seeks to escape the terrifying reality of human history, to make some sense of events, to hope for something better (an afterlife? a redemptive life? remembrance?) than what we have. And most of all, a majority of humans refuse to accept that the universe, the world, god(s), are utterly indifferent to our plight. But this is only the beginning.

One of Goya's most disturbing etchings, *El sueño de la razón produce monstruos,* shows a learned man sleeping at his desk, dreaming of irrational monsters. The etching has long been a coda for my course on the terror of history, and it is, in a sense, also a symbolic image for this book. Two translations of the title are possible from the original Spanish. One is that the sleep of reason produces monsters, meaning that when we cease to be rational (that is, when reason sleeps), irrational monsters come to the surface. In many respects, this interpretation of Goya's etching is the one closer to a long tradition in Spanish letters, harkening back to Calderón de la Barca's extraordinary play, *Life is a Dream*, which raises central questions as to the nature of reality. The second reading of the caption, I believe closer to Goya's meaning and to my own understanding, is that reason's dreams conjure monsters. What do I mean by that?

Most of Western civilization is a continuous dialogue between reason and unreason. The periods in which reason

Figure 1. Francisco de Lucientes Goya (1746–1828), *El sueño de la razon produce monstruos* (The Sleep of Reason Produces Monsters), plate 43 from "Los Caprichos," etching and aquatint, originally published in 1799. Image courtesy The Art Archive.

seems to have held sway—Classical Athens, the Scientific Revolution, the Enlightenment, the Europe of the late nineteenth and early twentieth centuries or the Belle Époque—were always accented by latent irrationality, religious fanaticism, and peculiar beliefs. It seems that Goya was absolutely right, and that the more we seem to embrace reason, the more irrationally we dream. If I am allowed to draw an example from not-so-recent popular culture, the iconic science-fiction film *Forbidden Planet* (a movie that is a loose rendering of Shakespeare's *The Tempest*) forcefully depicts the darker side of reason: a civilization so committed to the rational life that their dreams (their Ids in the pseudo-Freudian parlance of the movie's script) created monsters that eventually destroyed all life on the planet. Examples from the past also abound. We have long identified Classical Athens as the cradle of Western reason, but we should not be surprised that Plato, perhaps the most influential philosopher in Western thought, wrote his dialogues while Bacchic celebrations and mystery devotions (Orphic rituals, the cult of Demeter, and other such quasi-mystical practices) took place in Athens, or that Athens kept a human scapegoat ready to be sacrificed if things went too wrong in the city. Plato's most signal works were written shortly after Athens' defeat at the hands of Sparta and from a clear Spartanophile perspective. The Athenians, our standard paragons of democracy and enlightenment, had, after all, imposed a rather imperialist, oppressive, and not too rational, rule on its allies. They were also committed to an unmitigated misogyny, one of the aspects of Athenian society that Plato most severely criticized. This, that is Athenian imperialism, was, in turn, one of the causes of the Peloponnesian War and of the eventual demise of the Athenian empire. We tend to forget that it was Athenian democracy that executed Socrates, Plato's beloved teacher and the protagonist in almost all of his dialogues. Political liberty does not necessarily result in rational deeds.

The Scientific Revolution that transformed European thought in the sixteenth and seventeenth centuries was paralleled by the untold cruelties of religious warfare and the savagery of the witch craze. The same people who zealously advanced science were firm believers in the existence of witches and complicit in their destruction. The dazzling achievements and elegance of the Belle Époque in *fin-de-siècle* Western Europe, with its rational and beautiful art and architecture, was nurtured by European imperialism and the exploitation of colonial empires. Vienna's great cultural achievement paralleled the election of a vitriolic anti-Semitic mayor. It ended in the unprecedented (for the age) killing and destruction of World War I. In our own times, in this age of revolutionary technological breakthroughs and expanded university education, large segments of the population in the United States firmly believe that the end of times is imminent and that the selected few (which, of course, always includes them) will experience a "rapture" and be taken directly into the presence of god. Even more depressing is the fact that in a debate among Republican candidates for the presidential election in 2008, almost one third of the ten candidates running declared in public that they did not accept Darwin's theory of evolution, while some of the leading candidates advocated torture as a "rational" way to deal with terrorists. One should not be too harsh. It is perhaps after all part of the human drama that to live a rational life without fear is rare, and that what we call rationality and irrationality are part of the normal pendulum-swing of human existence. The terror of history is all around us, gnawing endlessly at our sense of, and desire for, order. It undermines, most of all, our hopes.

Writing History and Explaining Its Terror

Walter Benjamin, one of the most provocative thinkers of the first half of the twentieth century, committed suicide on the Spanish border with Vichy France in the fall of 1940. Fleeing Nazi Germany and denied transit through Spain on his way to freedom, Benjamin chose to end his life rather than to return to Germany and face the increasing persecution of Jews and others that led, in just a short span of time, to the horrors of the Holocaust. In one of his most thoughtful pieces—a short entry in his *Theses on the Philosophy of History*—Benjamin evokes a series of images that powerfully illuminate the critical vision of various twentieth-century intellectuals and that inspired the main themes of this book.

In a lapidary critique of historicism, Benjamin reflects on the meaning of culture and the writing of history. Not only is history written by the victors, he argues—an idea that seems self-evident in this age of spinning the news and managing public opinion—but, as he powerfully states: "There is no document of civilization which is not at the same time a document of barbarism."[1] Every cultural achievement, every iconic monument that stands as an example to the greatness of civilization has been created at a price. The price is injustice, oppression, inequality, war, and other barbarities that turn our individual and collective histories into what Hegel, describing history, once called "the slaughter bench of humanity." This is why Benjamin calls on all of us, historians and non-historians alike, to "brush history against the grain" and to write a different kind of account, one that deepens our

---

[1] Walter Benjamin, *Illuminations: Essays and Reflections*, ed. Hannah Arendt (New York: Schoken Books, 1968) 256.

understanding of the suffering of victims and losers, one that seeks to reveal the interstices of resistance and pain.

Benjamin's gloomy image is further accentuated in his moving allegory of the "angel of history." Having seen a painting by Klee entitled *Angelus Novus*—a rather odd painting, depicting a threatening and phantasmagorical vision (fig. 2)— Benjamin tells us that he likes to think of it as the angel of history.

> This is how one pictures the angel of history. His face is turned towards the past. Where we perceive a chain of events, he sees one single catastrophe which keeps piling wreckage upon wreckage and hurls it in front of his feet. The angel would like to stay, awaken the dead, and make whole what has been smashed. But a storm is blowing from Paradise; it has got caught in his wings with such violence that the angel can no longer close them. This storm irresistibly propels him into the future to which his back is turned, while the pile of debris before him grows skyward. This storm is what we call progress.[2]

Benjamin's indictment of progress and, by extension, of the Enlightenment project invites us to look at the flip side of history, at the chasm between official celebrations and harsh quotidian realities, and to become aware of the terrors and catastrophes that beset us at every step in our lives. It also invites us to reflect on the reality that our continuous celebration of Western technological advances and political order has been achieved through the continuous projection of power beyond our borders, by endless wars, and by systemic injustice and inequality.

[2] Benjamin, 257–58.

Figure 2. Paul Klee (1879–1940), *Angelus Novus,* 1920. Indian ink, color chalk, and brown wash on paper. Image courtesy The Israel Museum, Jerusalem, Israel / Carole and Ronald Lauder, New York / The Bridgeman Art Library. © 2010 Artists Rights Society (ARS), New York / VG Bild-Kunst, Bonn.

As social and political communities, we are constantly assailed by the unpredictability and cruelty of historical events. From the carnage of World War II to the nuclear terror of the Cold War to the events and aftermath of September 11, 2001 to new debilitating forms of warfare, we have been shaken again and again in our sense of security. On September 11 thousands of people died, parts of lower Manhattan were either destroyed or badly damaged, and the carnage and symbolic meaning of the targets chosen by the terrorists had a cumulative impact on most Americans and on many people abroad. One of the outcomes was that the terrorist attacks overthrew briefly, as they were intended to do, any sense of order. The act, unexpected for most people, undermined the very foundation of trust in the ability of governments and/or systems of belief to protect us or to foresee and thwart such deeds. Even if it did this only very briefly, the impact of September 11 also led to initial widespread support for unjust wars, internal restrictive and oppressive measures that may be a permanent legacy of 9/11, and a conflict with Iraq and Afghanistan already beyond its tenth year as I write these pages. The war has inflicted and continues to inflict an unspeakable toll on an innocent Iraqi and Afghan population and has cost a steadily climbing number of American casualties in both war theaters.

This is nothing new. Throughout human history unexpected catastrophes have shaken peoples' trust in rulers and beliefs, yielding harsh consequences. In fourteenth-century medieval Western Europe, to cite one example, severe famines, plagues, and wars often exposed the inability of monarchs and church dignitaries to provide solace to the population or to remedy disasters. The inefficacy of royal measures or religious rituals fueled the anxieties of the populace and led them to seek answers elsewhere: in flights of religious fervor, in apocalyptic and revolutionary outbursts, and in scapegoating the less fortunate. Their rulers also saw war as an option, and for more than a hundred years, France and England battered each other on the battlefield. In our own times, as the case of Iraq so clearly shows, modern governments have sought to respond to crisis by striking perceived or constructed enemies in ceaseless acts of violence.

From antiquity to the recent past, those in power have sought to protect their status by providing palliatives for uncertainty and disaster. Authority has often been projected in elaborate demonstrations (royal entries, religious processions, public executions, and the like) aimed at providing distraction from present evils and as didactic reminders of the social hierarchy and the unassailability of constituted power. Processions and spectacles—that is, the re-enactment of religious beliefs and the secular display of power (often a combination of both)—may go a long way toward assuaging fear and providing escape from the terror of history and the vicissitudes of historical events. But this is not always the case. There are moments—too frequent for our individual and collective comfort—when the routines of everyday life, the enduring presence of power, and the semblance of order are obliterated. Then the old trusted explanations and support systems are not enough.

Beyond extraordinary events or historical catastrophes "that pile skyward at the feet of the angel of history," the existential questions about why and how we live and what is our place in the universe remain crucial and agonizing for all thinking women and men. Deep within, we are aware of the uncertainty of life and the elusiveness of answers. The Greeks knew this long ago. Their most pessimistic take on the quandaries of human existence is best summarized in Sophocles' laconic but powerful line: "Not to be born is, past all prizing, best," a thought glossed brilliantly by Nietzsche in *The Birth of Tragedy* to the effect that, if you have the misfortune of being born, then it is best to die at an early age.

The choices are stark indeed. One choice leads us to accepting the world as we find it and trying to make the best of it by forceful and conscious acts of self-deception or denial. That is, being all along aware of Sophocles' dictum, we nonetheless embrace life and choose to live rather than never to be born (an act over which, after all, we have no control). The conundrum presented by this option is old indeed. In the *Odyssey,* one of Western culture's foundational texts, Odysseus, the indefatigable traveler and seeker of new knowledge, descends into Hades where he meets, among many Greek worthies, Achilles, the proud king of the dead. Achilles, who chose a short and heroic life over a long and mediocre one, now bemoans his demise. Praised by Odysseus and told not to "grieve at your death," Achilles responds with revealing words: "... not to make light of death, illustrious Odysseus.... I would rather work the soil as a serf on hire to some landless impoverished peasant than be king of all these lifeless dead."[3]

So much for the glorious death! The other choice in front of us is ignorance: to live, as many people in the world do today not by their own choice, a subhuman existence, to live an unreflected life. In this type of life, scrambling not to die of hunger or not to be killed in meaningless wars or mindless violence—think of the ongoing mass killings, mutilations, and the like carried out by drug cartels in Mexico—become the driving goal of one's life. There is of course always the option of ending one's existence, an idea not unlike Camus' assurance that suicide is the last form of self-control in a cruel universe. Yet Achilles' utterance just cited above is a powerful

[3] *The Odyssey* (London: Penguin Books, 2003) 152.

reminder that putting an end to things, trying to escape with that final act, though seemingly easy, is indeed very difficult. We strive mightily, whether consciously or unconsciously, to live.

This is in spite of the fact that the burdens we face in our individual lives are many. If I may borrow from a non-Western story, in the life of Siddhartha Gautama, the Buddha, the young prince awakened to his quest for enlightenment by successive encounters with other people's illness, old age, and death. Moved by the awareness that humans will most likely experience all three, he chose to be enlightened; he chose a path of action and meditation that would lead him not to be born again and again in the endless wheel of life, not to experience life in endless stages of reincarnation. For Westerners, this idea of nothingness as the goal of one's life is a hard pill to take.

And yet, like the Buddha, we are also deeply aware of the frailty and arbitrariness of our lives, of illnesses, aging, and death. Suspecting or knowing that there is probably no meaning or order in the universe, we combat this dark perspective by continuously making meaning, by imposing order on our chaotic and savage past, by constructing explanatory schemes that seek to justify and elucidate what is essentially inexplicable. These half-hearted attempts to explain the inexplicable and to make sense of human cruelty are what we call "history." It is the writing of history itself. Take the twentieth century, a century of extraordinary technological and scientific achievements. It was also a century of such horror and carnage that the mere telling of one act of genocide after another, of one war after another, of our nuclear nightmare, of untold ethnic cleansing, religious strife, and continuous racism and misogyny should make any rational human being shudder. And the twentieth-first century does not seem promising either.

Escaping History

One can describe human attempts to deal with disaster in myriad ways. A few selected categories will serve as a framework for these reflections. Johan Huizinga, a great and perceptive Dutch historian who wrote about the morbidity and angst of the "autumn of the Middle Ages," posited three ways in which late medieval people dealt with the uncertainties of their lives: religion, possessions and material goods, and aesthetic or artistic yearnings. In other words, men and women at the "waning" of an age sought relief either through belief (in a whole variety of orthodox and heterodox forms), the life of the senses, and/or through culture and the pursuit of the beautiful. We can apply Huizinga's typology to our own lives and historical experiences and place our discussion within these categories.

RELIGION

Religion or religious experiences, in its (or their) many different variations means essentially the way in which one (or the many) places oneself in the hands of god (or the gods). Religion posits the terrors besetting one's own personal life and the weight of collective history as part of a divine plan and as the sum total of inscrutable but always wise actions of an all-powerful, all-knowing deity (or deities). The religious man or woman will often find great solace in belief. Though god's (or the gods') actions often seem inexplicable and cruel, there is always the reassuring belief that the deity knows why such things need to happen. There is, after all, a higher purpose. In the end, all events, awful and good, form part of an overarching sacred project in which we all play a part.

Let's not discount religion. Having attended a religious ceremony recently in which a group of young men took their initial vows into the Society of Jesus, I, who claim to be a devoted atheist, was strangely swept by the heightened emotions present in the very crowded church. It was a very moving experience, and, as I was leaving the ceremony, I had to remind myself once more that some historians (myself most guilty of this) fail to acknowledge the power of belief only at their peril. Religion, after all, has created, and continues to create, meaning for a significant part of humanity. It promises, at least in the Western world, redemption and a life after. It guarantees eternal rewards to those who endure the terror and remain faithful to a prescribed set of doctrines or rituals. It provides, with extraordinary clarity and assurance for the believer, what is, in fact, a form of life. Religious beliefs have often been deployed and articulated—sometimes in rather peculiar forms—to deal with the social, economic, cultural, and political transformations of Western Europe and the anxieties that these changes brought to the minds and hearts of Europeans from antiquity to the present. Often, however, religious answers, as interpreted by those in power or by those dissenting from that power, led to persecution and strife.

This is indeed a question worth pondering: Is religion, in its effort to emplot human life within a divine scheme and to emphasize the superiority of one set of beliefs over another, one of the main causes of warfare and injustice? Norman Housley's book, *Religious Warfare*, adroitly raises the issue of the role of religion in some of the most violent episodes in late medieval and early modern European history. The evidence seems to point to a linkage between exalted religious beliefs and violence, between uncompromising faith and persecution. In that sense, religious violence is, in a bizarre and perverse fashion, yet one more way of dealing with the uncertainties of the world. When a man is ready to blow himself up and take enemies along because the act will lead him straight to paradise, what we are witnessing is an extreme form of belief that, although grounded in long traditions of sacrifice, religious martyrdom, and historical realities, is, by its very nature, ahistorical, a form of escape from history and from the world as presently constituted. We do not even need to use contemporary examples to make this point. History is filled with such extreme forms of behavior: from Christian martyrdom in pagan Rome, to the fierce and suicidal defense of believers at Canudos (see chapter 2) to other forms of religious behavior. Religion explains the inexplicable. Many however do not accept the explanations of religion. Many, including myself, do not believe. Some, even though believing in god (or the gods), have also resolutely and sometimes even bitterly turned their backs on organized forms of religion or religious rituals. The problem perhaps is not belief per se. The problem is intolerant forms of religious belief.

EMBRACING THE MATERIAL WORLD

Many of those who have lost their faith, or who never had one to begin with, have developed ways just as intricate as those created by religious individuals to keep at bay the terrifying specter of history. Throughout human existence, many have embraced the material world as a means of keeping down the gnawing suspicion that we live in a Sisyphean universe in which, with great effort, we roll a heavy stone up a hill only to have it immediately roll down to the starting point. By acquiring material goods and accumulating wealth, we often seek to provide an answer to the quandaries of history and life. In the Western world today, most of our aspirations, thoughts, and fears have been ameliorated or exorcized by the ephemeral possession of goods and the commodification of our daily lives. But owning things is inherently impermanent and leads to greater fears: losing what we have, or not having enough (most people never have enough money, enough paintings, enough books, enough rare wines, etc.) to truly quell existential fears. It is never enough.

What other paths are there? There is the life of sensory and sensual pleasure, of permanent intoxication—Baudelaire argued that one must go through life intoxicated (though he meant it in an aesthetic sense). As attractive as this alternative may seem as a release from the burdens of human existence, our bodies will not endure a life of dissipation and intoxication for very long, even if one ignores the social and ethical consequences of a permanent state of intoxication. In the same vein, love—by which I mean here sexual, physical love and not its romanticized and aestheticized form that is far more part of art than of the here-and-now world—also intoxicating and consuming, and work, which is the main and most consuming activity for most people in the Western world, provide temporary solace from the harsh realities of the world. As to work, this would include not just physical activity, but also intellectual and/or creative processes that although also a form or "work" seek to come to terms with history in a different fashion. In the end, creating and maintaining routines (whether in our quotidian activities, lovemaking, or work), we establish recognizable patterns in the fabric of our individual lives and fold them into the collective destiny of our communities. By making love, working, owning things, spending money, building careers, getting fellowships (such as the one that partly allows me to write this book), we gain membership in a larger community. We give meaning to our lives. We make some sense of the universe, even without religion.

THE PURSUIT OF BEAUTY

There are those who, rejecting religion or refusing to embrace the material world, build their lives around the pursuit of knowledge, art, and beauty as an end unto itself. "The unexamined life," Plato argued famously, supposedly quoting Socrates, "is not worth living." And indeed the pursuit of "the beautiful and the good," both of these categories in their full Platonic sense—but also as naively articulated in our pedagogical programs and ethical ideals—can certainly become a different kind of secular religion. Scholars, artists, and aesthetes may wish to think, and do most often (see chapter 4), that their approach is superior, or that it is more worthwhile and less delusional than the pursuit of religion, hedonism, or intoxication. I may even say that art as an escape is probably more useful and far less threatening than the other two options. After all, scholars and artists do not go around killing people because they do not like or believe in Klee's artistic value or agree or disagree with Descartes' *Discourse on Method*. We do get at times vitriolic in our comments and reviews of the works of others, but it never leads to widespread bloodshed, and only rarely to physical violence. In the end, however, all three ways briefly discussed above—religion, material and sensory aspirations, and aesthetics—remain forms of escape from the reality of the world and the cruelty of history.

All of these approaches—and there are of course others —aim at coming to terms with our awareness of mortality, with the fragility of our lives, with the ephemeral nature of our well-being and happiness. The Greeks, who in the West understood the tragedy of life in a keener fashion than anyone else, tell us in their open-ended myths and engaging stories about this quandary. Herodotus, the great storyteller, describes Solon's voyages in the Aegean after he had given a constitution to Athens. Stopping in the kingdom of Lydia, he is given hospitality by King Croesus, reputed to be the richest man alive. Asked by Croesus who is the happiest man—and the king, of course, equates, as many do in our society today, wealth and power with happiness—Solon embarks on elaborate stories about two athletes and a warrior who, through their sacrifices and honorable deaths, gained the admiration of their fellow citizens and posthumous fame. The king is puzzled indeed. After all, these worthies were no longer among the living. How happy could they really be? Much later, as he waits to be burned alive by the conquering Persians, he comes to a full understanding of the poignant reality that we cannot call our lives happy until the very moment of death. We live, as it were, always on the edge of the abyss, and when we think we are happy and at peace, as individuals and as communities, awful things may be waiting just around the corner. Yet, though the Greeks knew this—as do we in the recesses of our minds—they turned their backs, as we do too, on Sophocles' uncompromising admonition that it would have been better never to have been born. It is, as noted earlier, in human nature to cling to life, to hope against hope. We make meaning. We write history. In various ways we seek to escape from the terrors of our individual and collective lives. We want both to escape history and, in my case, to write it as well.

Time and History

But these ideas and categories of forms of escape from history are just thin layers, a palimpsest over which other themes are written and rewritten again and again. Behind the conscious efforts to create or imagine ways that may permit us to live in the world "as is" and to endure the cumulative burdens of history, there is a deeper and far more troublesome awareness. An earlier reader of this book commented perceptively on my role as "notary," that is, as a recorder of these reactions to history, as a somewhat detached narrator. Seeking to offer explanations, retelling events, I have failed to note fully the extent to which I am complicit in these unfoldings and representations of history and how my "reflections" become entangled in the process of my being in history. Writing about the different paths that lead us away from history cannot be done from the outside. I am, as would anyone be who engages in this task or in the writing of history, implicated in the actual process that I seek to describe. I have been, I am, far more of an actor here than my impersonal narrator may lead you to believe.

In writing this, I have the powerful sense that I have not conveyed exactly or clearly what it is that I mean to say. It is quite difficult to write about something in which one is a participant without having the "I" that writes intervene, shape, distort what one is attempting to express. This is one of the reasons I have inserted autobiographical vignettes throughout the book. I have not done so because I think my life is so interesting that it should be told; rather, I do so as a reminder to the reader, and to myself as well, that we are all participants in this process. The same reader, a cherished friend, also insightfully noted that when I reflect on the terror of history or write, as I do in succeeding pages of Benjamin's "angel of history," I make a crucial mistake. History, as he pointed out, has no agency. People do. Historians do. The terrors that befall humanity have been (and are) described, rendered into words, analyzed, and bent into place by historians. This continuous recapturing of past events, the reshaping of them according to our own particular ideological leanings is the ever-evolving context in which individuals and communities journey through history. The muse of history, in her simplest incarnation the attempt to memorialize the past, is always neutral. What historians and other scholars do is never so.

There is a further point that needs to be considered. Far more relevant than the uneasy relation of historians to history is the relation of humans to time. Long ago Augustine of Hippo engaged in one of the most thorough and insightful discussions of time. In Book XI of his *Confessions*, Augustine sought to understand the relation between eternity and time, between god and his creation. For my purpose here, two points are significant. One is the relation of time to history; the second is the link of others and myself to time. Following a reader's suggestion, I argue therefore that Santillana's famous dictum that those who do not know history are condemned to repeat it is blatantly false. In the chapters to come I have eschewed a chronological narrative in favor of conveying my own "phenomenological account," that is, my own narrow and limited experience of history, both as thought and as lived. This is, though I did not realize it fully until it was pointed out to me, a confession. But it is also my own attempt to place myself within history and in time. In that sense, history here is understood not as pedagogy, in Santillana's sense, but as reflections on experiences. To write or to live history is to encompass those narrated moments that were once the past, present, and future. Thus, I wish to note that it is precisely this shifting sense of time that I seek to capture. A sense of time in which the present is always becoming the past, in which the present is always giving birth to an undetermined future. A sense in which the future soon ceases to be and becomes both present and past.

There is something terrifying in our awareness of time, or, to be more precise, in our awareness of the passing of time. Not only is time puzzling and difficult to understand in a philosophical sense, as Augustine's brilliant grappling with the subject shows, but time, as experienced by humans, is terrifying indeed. When you get to be as old as I am at present—and I will be older still when you read this—you become aware of how swiftly time runs. Long ago, when I was young, it did not seem to move. Now it seems like a huge waterfall, moving incessantly to some appointed death. I am, of course, not saying anything new. Among Goya's striking dark paintings, there is a ghastly one of Saturn (Chronos) eating his children. It is a pictorial representation of one of Ancient Greece's most telling myths. The god Chronos (time) devours his children out of fear that, as fate has predicted, one of them will overthrow him. And so does Chronos devour all of us. As I retell stories about mystics, messianic figures, those who seek the pleasures of the body, those who embrace beauty, one common tread runs through their collective wishes: to obliterate time, to stop change, to end time or to achieve, through prayer, purgation, ecstatic physical joy, or aesthetic redemption that timelessness that would take us beyond history and decay.

Reflections on the Terror of History

What I hope to accomplish in this enterprise is to construct a narrative that functions as a "reflection" or exploration of the human condition, using specific historical examples to illustrate how religion, material concerns, and aesthetic yearnings have partially driven and shaped the contours of our responses to the harshness of history. In doing so, we should note the palliative measures that are plotted by those in positions of power as a distraction, and the diverse forms of escape that are, themselves, ways of resisting history and the established order. For they are not mutually exclusive. What begins as an attempt to shape society and systems of beliefs to benefit one social class may lead to unpredictable consequences. For example, Carnival, often heavily scripted from the late Middle Ages to the present for the benefit of those on top, could, and did, devolve into rebellion and resistance from below. When a town was swept by Carnival fever, the ordinary flow of time was suspended—as still happens today. Carnival creates a timeless space in which to ignore the continuous devolution of history, the inequity of social and economic differences.

The challenge of writing a book such as this is an exciting and difficult one. This is, of course, not intended to be a typical history book, addressing particular aspects of the social and cultural history of the West. Instead, it is a reflection on human reactions to disaster and on the ways in which we, collectively and individually, cope with crisis (social, structural, as well as existential). What I seek to capture is the ever present tension, to return to an earlier comment, between Sophocles' bitter statement in *Oedipus at Colonus* that "not to be born is, past all prizing, best," and Camus' stark and courageous (or pessimistic) acceptance of life in the face of the indifference of the universe (and history) in *The Stranger*. In the interstices created by the tension between these two difficult choices, human beings formulated, and continue to formulate, diverse ways of escaping from the "terror of history." Or to put it more bluntly, when faced with these two choices—one denying existence, the other arguing for its acceptance despite its meaninglessness—we seek to make sense of the world through varieties of religious experiences, by embracing the material world, by the quest for the beautiful or wisdom, or by a motley combination of all of these methods. Moreover, a distinction should be drawn between mass movements and individual responses to the pressures of history, though undoubtedly individuals in this account are chosen as examples only because their actions led to collective withdrawals from, or resistance to, history.

In the preface and in this first chapter, I have sought to explore how men and women have shaped and responded to history in the West over *la longue durée* and, specifically, to explain what I mean when I write about and discuss "the terror of history." Reflecting on these issues, I aim to understand or try to make sense of how historians—and that includes myself—have sought to explicate the past and make sense of historical experiences. In chapter 2, I examine religion (both orthodox and heterodox spirituality, including millennial agitation). These religious experiences come in a diversity of forms. They range from mysticism to heresy to millennial agitation, esoteric forms of belief, and the widespread acceptance of the supernatural. For example, from antiquity to the present, one of the signal individual and collective responses to social, economic, and cultural crises has been mysticism. Mysticism is an exalted form of religion, in which the mystic claims that he or she has become one with god. Though mystics are relatively few in number, they play a unique role in reinforcing religious beliefs and in reassuring their contemporaries of the validity of their claims of oneness with god. Few religions, certainly few Western religions, can prosper without mysticism. The mystical experience, described and claimed as true by numerous mystics (and, more significantly, accepted by many others as true), was a religious state open to the very few; yet it inspired the many. Mysticism was, and remains, a highly individual pursuit; yet, once they had achieved union with god, most mystics in the West, as shall be seen, took a hand in the affairs of the world and strove mightily to transform the society in which they lived. By doing so, they provided solace to those who accepted the validity of such experiences.

Mystics came in two forms: orthodox and heterodox. Both played a significant role in the formulation of escapes from history. Not unlike mystics, heretics and those who embraced millennial dreams shared a commitment to their own vision of the world and of faith. To hold heretical views or to preach the end of time in medieval and early modern Europe was a risky business. The upholding of heterodox beliefs in Western Europe even into the present could, and often did, have dire consequences. It could lead to death or to exclusion from society. Yet heresies and apocalyptic expectations were seldom individual activities. Most often heretics and believers in the millennium formed groups of men and women ranging from a handful to thousands. They joined together in a common assertion that either the Church was upholding mistaken beliefs or that the end of time was at hand. The real strength of these movements resided in the strong bonds that were created among their members and in the sense of belonging and identity that these beliefs engendered.

Unlike mystics, heretics, and millenarian groups, others delved into a series of esoteric practices—magic, alchemy, astrology, and hermeticism—practices that, at least in the Middle Ages and the early modern period, straddled the worlds of religion and science. These pursuits were open only to a few scholars, although some forms of magic had wide popular appeal. These types of knowledge, therefore, required unique dedication, faith, and secretiveness. There was no desire to convert others or to reach the masses. Whether in search of power or patronage in the case of some magicians and astrologers, or whether in search of arcane knowledge that would reveal the secrets of existence, those who practiced these arts often embraced their craft with a passion and commitment that replicated the religious experience. In many ways, magic, astrology, alchemy, and hermeticism functioned as forms of religion. They sought to deny—or accept—the terror of history by recognizing the inexorable, fatal, and sometimes beneficial, influence of the stars, and by seeking to manage that influence through amulets, incantations, and arcane lore.

Finally, witchcraft or, more accurately, the witch craze that swept Europe from the late Middle Ages to the late seventeenth century, was a popular phenomenon. Rooted in rural beliefs but defined by learned discourse, the alleged practice of witchcraft transgressed social and educational boundaries. It linked the rarefied culture of the elite with folk traditions. As inscribed in the dominant culture by normative texts—most notably the *Malleus Malificarum* (or *The Hammer of Witches*)—the persecution and execution of witches, a large number of them older women, created a convenient outlet for the fears and anxieties of most people in early modern Europe. Fed by misogyny and kindled by a context of dramatic social, economic, cultural, and political changes, the identification, hunting, burning, and hanging of witches diverted the attention of most of the population from the harsh realities of the world and squarely placed blame on witches for the misfortunes of the age. The witch then joined a long list of scapegoats—the Jew, the leper, the Muslim, the heretic, the homosexual, and others on the margins of society—who, at one time or another, played (and continue to play) the role of victim in the unfolding of human history.

In chapter 3, "The World of Matter," I examine the material embrace of the world (from the accumulation of capital and property to the long philosophical tradition that emphasizes the tangible in the universe and human life). There are myriad aspects to explore here. The material world held (and holds) a powerful grip on untold numbers of individuals. The reaction of many in Western Europe to the onslaught of the Black Death, as told in graphic detail by Boccaccio and others, is just one example of the way in which the embracing of revelry, intoxication, and debauchery as a choice against the misfortunes of historical events has played a role in human existence. The Marquis de Sade's writings and his actual life provide a window into alternate ways of seeing and escaping history.

Festivals, Carnival, and sports, so often used in unhealthy ways to assert one's national identity and patriotism, are some of the forms of escape chosen by many in society in the face of despair. Bacchic celebrations, even with their deeply religious elements, were another way to confront the weight of history through sensorial escape. A study of Carnival and Carnivalesque celebrations through time is an excellent example of the role of the body and of celebration in human history. Similarly, sexuality, in its many varieties, has been an important way of disarming the terror of history. Utopias constructed around sexual promiscuity and myths of plentiful eating and no work, as in the land of Cockaigne, for example, have played and continue to play a significant role in human experience.

These models were not limited to just the fantasies of some writers or the imagination of starving peasants. They had actual counterparts in utopian experiments in antiquity (Plato's attempt to establish a community in Sicily along the lines of his *Republic*), in early modern Europe (Campanella's experiments; the Jesuit utopian establishments in Paraguay), and in our contemporary world (the Oneonta experiments, Skinnerian communities, and other such millenarian attempts).

The United States was crawling with utopian communities in the nineteenth century, and some of these have survived into the present. Such exercises *against* history are quite common in the Western experience.

In chapter 4, "The Lure of Beauty and Knowledge," I emphasize culture, that is, cultural production and aesthetic concerns as a response to historical crisis. So is, in a sense, this book. Writing, art, music are creative forms of sublimating uncertainties about one's life and historical role. Not all artists seek to escape history. Some seek to validate it, but certainly a large number have sought to deny history through the production of the beautiful, the shocking, the offensive. Writers, existentialist writers most notably, sought to abolish and to deny the teleologies and certainties of the historical process, and wrote as a response to real crises—World War I, World War II, the rise of industrial society. Baudelaire's dictum (quoted earlier) expresses perfectly that blending of material escape (the state of permanent intoxication) with aesthetic longings. This could range from the uncompromising or depressing options offered by Camus and Kafka to the solace of romance (from Chretièn de Troyes's imagined Arthurian court to Sir Walter Scott's or Dumas' novels). Science fiction and fantasy are good examples of the way in which literature, film, and art often seek to provide a more controlled universe in opposition to the existing harsh reality of the world. In Tolkien, C. S. Lewis, and J. K. Rowlings' books, the clear distinction between good and evil, though rooted in historical allusions, always provides for a comforting denouement. Who has not escaped the troubles of everyday life in the pages of the *Silmarillion*, *The Lord of the Rings*, or in an imagined Narnia or Hogwarts?

To these three overarching themes—forms of religious experiences, the embrace of the material, and aesthetic escape—

we can add subsidiary sub-themes (to be woven into the narrative): violence (scapegoating, the witch craze, the theatricality of punishment in the form of inquisitorial autos-de-fé or public executions), Eros, and romantic imaginings. Yet I insist once again in my refusal to make any universalist claims. Rather, one of my arguments is that although human beings everywhere face more or less the same challenges from history, the ways in which the angst of the human condition has been, and is, addressed remains always grounded in specific cultural contexts and individual experiences, and that these responses change—in their outward manifestations—over time. In writing this, I realize the trap into which I have willingly walked. While individuals and communities seek to escape history, they often do so in forms and from within contexts that are deeply historical in nature. In some respects, not too far removed from certain aspects of Marx's view of the past, history is continually subverting itself. History thus has to be seen as part of a dialectical process, something like Marx's class struggle. Unlike Marx, I see the conflict as arising from our desire to abolish history and our inability to do so. Unlike Marx, I do not ever expect the end of class struggle or the advent of utopia, whether religious, material, or aesthetic. Unlike Marx, I do not see a future in which history comes to an end: the Golden Country of Orwell's *1984*. The future, I fear, may be as dark as the present.

This does not mean that there is no forward movement, no progress. Technical progress there has been. In fact, the explosion in technology is so intense that it accelerates time all around us. Nor does this mean that we should throw our hands into the air and give up. All to the contrary, it is only a greater incentive to fight on.

Focusing on examples that show extreme human responses to disasters, these vignettes will be drawn from all historical periods, but with emphasis on the ancient world, the Middle Ages, and early modern Europe. Some of the mystery religions or cults—Bacchic celebrations, the maintenance of an official scapegoat in Classical Athens—serve as apt counterpoints to the usual emphasis on reason with which we identify Golden Age Athens. As to the Middle Ages and the early modern period, some of the best-known forms of millenarian agitation and heterodox religious practices provide fertile ground for my exploration. I am thinking in particular of the heady mixture of religion and social unrest that characterized the English peasant risings of 1381 and the Hussite wars. The great German peasant uprising in the early sixteenth century and its aftermath would yield abundant material. Yet, our contemporary world also deserves attention. The collective suicide of the Heaven's Gate cult members in San Diego, more than two decades ago, also provides a vivid and dramatic example of the denial of history, or, at least, of specific normative types of history.

In this vein, utopian texts such as Campanella's *The City of the Sun* (which can be placed within a revolutionary social context in early modern Calabria), or descriptions of Carnival and its counterpart, inquisitorial trials, serve to draw together forms of exalted religiosity, a culture of violence, and social inversion. Some mystical texts, such as *The Little Flowers,* may prove very useful as well. Along those lines, the life of Francis of Assisi provides us a wonderful example of the individual who seeks to confront changes in the social and economic contexts in which he lived. Francis' response to questions of property, salvation, the material world, nature, and man's relation to God went beyond the experiences of a lone individual. His example ignited a radical reinterpretation of the Gospel's message of poverty and Christianity's social responsibility, leading to new radical ways of seeing the world among the Fraticelli and other radical Franciscans from shortly after Francis' death in 1226 into the early modern period.

I would also like to draw on other lesser-known examples. I am thinking in particular of the movement known as Sebastianism in Portugal and parts of the Portuguese empire. The idea that King Sebastián would return from the battlefields of North Africa, where he was killed or lost, to lead Portugal to an apocalyptic and redemptive destiny—leading to the end of history—had immense repercussions in sixteenth- and seventeenth-century political life. Echoes of these millenarian ideas appear in the rebellion of the Canudos in late nineteenth-century Brazil (in the state of Bahía), a wonderful story worth retelling and explicating. One could go on providing examples and identifying avenues for research, but the time has come to discuss these matters in some detail.

❋ II ❋

Religion and the World to Come

___

As a child and an adolescent, I attended a private Catholic school, entertained, as did many of my schoolmates, thoughts of the priesthood, and even joined a small ascetic community. Reading Loyola's *Spiritual Exercises* and the life of St. Francis, fasting every Thursday, even refusing to drink any liquids on those days in the tropical setting of my youth, I thought I had grasped some deep understanding of the world and of my own spirituality. But my religion was, after all, that of Cuba. As such, my beliefs were always undermined by the sights and sounds of my sensuous homeland and by my coming of age in the midst of a revolution. A new and far more passionate "religious" feeling—revolutionary ideals—swept me along, as they did many of my friends and contemporaries, into an intense, though short-lived belief that we could create the kingdom of heaven on earth, and that equality, a kind of Franciscan "socialism," was possible. Like many people my age, I thought I could be an instrument, a participant in changing the world. Growing old is also the realization that as much as some of us may wish to do so, it is not to be. The world changes us instead. Or rather, if we are successful in carrying out some changes or impressing some of the students in our classes, the changes are individual and limited in scope. The larger and transformative changes have eluded us, or, at least, have eluded me.

Having thus grown up with this deeply felt religious fervor, I slowly lost my faith during my twenties and have remained for the last four decades a devoted atheist, though, as I mentioned in the previous chapter, I was caught completely unaware recently by the wave of feelings prompted by witnessing a taking of vows into the Jesuit order by one of my students and his colleagues. Nonetheless, here is my confession, so the reader knows what my biases and limitations are. Lack of belief in god, and most certainly mistrust of religion, does not mean that as a historian or a human being I do not understand and cannot be sympathetic (within limits of course) to the power of religious belief in shaping human existence or in providing solace, escape, and meaning to untold millions throughout the world. My lack of belief does not mean that I would, or should, be dismissive of religion's ability to shape historical events and discourse. We know that from many historical examples, and, in this particular instance, most vividly, from the widespread response to the onslaught of the Black Death in mid-fourteenth-century Europe. As we have seen, the first and most enduring reaction to the plague's carnage and to other similar catastrophes has been to see illness and natural or human-inflicted disasters as god's punishment on a wicked humanity. This act of affirmation—catastrophes are god's justified response to humankind's weakness, lack of faith, stubbornness, and many other of our reprehensible traits—has a very long pedigree in Western tradition.

In the Old Testament, a text that plays such a central role in the spiritual and cultural history of the West, we are taught, again and again, of god's wrath at the sins of his/her/its chosen people. Catastrophes, whether fire and brimstone, the destruction of entire cities à la Sodom and Gomorrah, plagues, the slaughtering of every first-born child, or endless wanderings in the desert, were part of god's manipulation of history and, thus, historical in nature. Of course, in the Christian West, processions, frequent masses, scourging of one's body (and sometimes that of others—as flagellants did in 1266 when the world was supposed to come to an end, or in the plague of 1348 when it almost seemed that it did) and other bizarre forms of expiation and repentance were (and remain) part and parcel of a vast repertory of propitiatory and atonement acts offered to god. This is of course not unique to Western experience, since in other cultures gods (or at least those speaking for god or the gods) expected and received more of the same.

Throughout the West, even to as late a date as today, religious observances and performances beyond the usual liturgical requirements of the religious year are aimed at holding the world together. Clearly, humanity as a whole is not deserving of god's protection. Prayer, certainly among Catholics, is a continuous negotiation with the godhead to prevent the annihilation of the world. Sometimes that is not enough and god allows or inflicts on humanity such horrors as the Holocaust, the Pol Pot genocide, and other such excesses perpetrated by one set of humans against other humans. Many of us of course think that these events emerge from particular social and cultural settings and have nothing to do with the transcendental. For many of us, these ghastly deeds are yet one more example of humans' cruelty to other humans and even, as Ivan Karamazov argued to his younger brother in Dostoevsky's great novel, of the absence or silence of god. Others however see them as god's just punishment on sinning and wicked humans. Thus, some fundamentalist preachers in the good old USA saw the spread of AIDS as god's revenge on an immoral society. In fact, one must admit that there are many in our country for whom the end of the world is not to be postponed or feared. Rather, it must be welcomed as part of a divine plan that will take the chosen few beyond history and time and condemn the rest of us to awful death and eternal damnation.

These exalted feelings of being freed of the world's burdens by god's will or by a superior intelligence's design (extraterrestrials) can assume bizarre and ahistorical aspects, such as the cult-like Heaven's Gate group. A group of middle-class, fairly well educated, and seemingly normal people in suburban San Diego of all places, a location as close to paradise in terms of climate and the bountifulness of material culture as you can get on this earth, engaged in extreme ascetic practices —including in some specific cases voluntary castration—and eventually committed collective suicide in expectation of being transported to a spaceship that was riding unseen and undetected behind a comet. And from this alleged spaceship, the group would be lifted to a higher level of consciousness. If this had happened in the Middle Ages (and some in that period actually thought of things like this, though of course without the spaceship), we would all be bemoaning the ignorance and superstitious nature of medieval people, but then strange things do happen in California.

Following along this same line of thought, many of the citizens of Münster in sixteenth-century Germany saw themselves as the godly in a sea of ungodly people. They saw their city as a radical utopian paradise, and their cause that of righteousness as they waited to be slaughtered by besieging armies. The poor victims of Jonestown in Guyana and the families in Waco, Texas, who followed the charismatic leadership of David Koresh, adhered to a rather common pattern of behavior among radical and fundamentalist religious groups.

If such extreme forms of behavior, a pattern of conduct quite common in the Western world and present also in the histories of non-Western people, were limited to a small fringe that made occasional sensational appearances in the news, we could dismiss them as an aberration, but in this country— which seems to ail from religious fervor far more than other secular Western societies—those who accept the literal meaning of the scriptures and hope fervently for a "rapture" represent a significant percentage of the population and wield a political influence that has led, to our great and long-term damage, to the election of someone like George Bush in two successive elections and to the successes of the so-called Tea Party in the last election.

Beyond these ramblings, the question remains: what are we to make of religion? I do not wish in this book to discuss the validity or illusory nature of religion (to borrow Freud's formulation). Debates on the existence or non-existence of god are a complete waste of time. Belief, often deeply and sincerely felt, is a personal way of seeing the world and one's place in that world. Science cannot disprove the existence of god (although it may show the irrationality of religion). Religion cannot disprove scientific thought. In the West, these two different ways of experiencing and explaining the world, as well as the place of men and women in it, parted company as early as the late thirteenth century—though the Greeks and Romans had gone farther along that road before Christianity reshaped the Western world. In the context of the nineteenth-century scientific revolution with it new paradigms of thought, Marx, Darwin, Freud, and others erected boundaries between "belief" and "knowledge"—boundaries that sometimes proved more porous than their makers had intended.

This is not a book about belief or against belief; nor is it an attack on religion. Rather, I beg the reader's permission to allow me to sever, at least for this reflection, one from the other, that is, to separate belief from the historical reality of religion. I further ask to be able to consider the varieties of religious experiences found through human history (mostly in the West) as historical phenomena. We must not forget that for the religious individual or group, human history and its manifold experiences emerge from the divine and that, viewed from this perspective, history becomes part of an over-arching religious discourse or narrative. But if we accept that religions, as separate from belief or the question of the exis-tence or nonexistence of god, result from specific structural contexts, then how does that fit into my argument that reli-gion is a form of escape from the terror of history? The an-swer is a simple one, and I hope that the examples that follow will resolve this apparent contradiction.

Religion, Power, and Politics

If history, as defined earlier, is our attempt to explain the ca-tastrophes that befall mankind, that pile of debris mounting sky high in front of the angel of history, and to try to make sense of these disasters, then, in many respects, escaping from history is also a form or resistance to history and to estab-lished lines of authority. Similarly, the act of historicizing the past and, in this particular case historicizing religion, is yet another form of escape. It functions as a way to bind history and religion within temporal frameworks. One cannot also proceed in this discussion without some reference to the re-lationship between religion and power, between religion and the most obvious manifestation of political power: war. Clearly, religious beliefs and observances are part of the normal un-folding of history. We have long known, for example, how religion underpins political authority, and vice versa. From the first written historical records of mankind to the religious symbols displayed in modern democracies today—think for example of the oath taken on the Bible by politicians and those sworn to serve on juries, the religious invocations in Congress, references to god in school pledges, and the like— religion and politics have long blended almost seamlessly into coherent structures of power.

In Rome not a negligible part of imperial authority derived from the emperor's role as *pontifex maximus*, the highest official of the formal state religion throughout the land. So did the "Mandate of Heaven" serve as a way to legitimate political power in second-millennium-BCE China. In medieval Western Europe most kings ruled by the "grace of god;" their power vested via elaborate ceremonies of anointment or crowning, or through even more extreme claims of royal thaumaturgical power (e.g., the claims that the kings of France and England could cure scrofula by the touch of their hands). There was no political power in the Western premodern world without god. There was no exercise of authority without the underpinning of religious structures, serving as intermediaries between the sacred and the world. But of course such links are still present in our contemporary world. Think of Franco's link to the Church in post–Civil War Spain or the ties of Bush and many other recently elected politicians—most of them born-again Christians—to the Christian fundamentalist Right. But even long before written records, archeological evidence, pictorial representations, and folklore tell us of the intertwining of religious symbolism, magical motifs, and daily life.

In the Western world, such a historical activity as warfare has been always closely related to religion. Reiterating Norman Housley's arguments, one could simply say that religion has been one of the main catalysts for warfare. One may modify this argument by stating that conflicts between religions or within one specific religion have led to fierce carnage. One only needs to think of the horrific religious wars that devastated most of Christian Europe in the sixteenth and first half of the seventeenth century, of the enduring conflicts between Shia and Sunni, between Muslims and Hindus, Muslims and Jews, or the still smoldering embers of Protestant-Catholic conflicts in Ireland (though a resolution seemed almost to have been at hand, thanks mostly to Ireland's new found— and soon lost—prosperity). Granted, many of these religious conflicts were, and are, also linked to issues of ethnicity, race, culture, and a multitude of other historical factors, but it is peculiar that most people's often preferred way of self-identification on our planet is religion. Far worse, the preferred way of identifying the enemy is also centered on religion, though, oddly enough, the most violent deeds are directed not at those who are quite different but at those who are close by or differ from our beliefs in only small ways. Russell Jacobi's forthcoming brilliant book on fraternal violence shows that wars are always harsher against a known enemy than an unknown one.

Spaniards in the Caribbean and in Mexico at the dawn of the early modern period always described themselves as Christians, while the natives whom they intended to subjugate, were identified as either infidel pagans or even Muslims. Their great temples were accordingly described as "mosques." In today's troubled world, politicians imprudently speak of the "clash of civilizations." This is a not-so-veiled code for religious differences and the fallacious argument that such differences cannot be easily accepted in a Christian world. Think of the ongoing debate about Europe's Christian identity or the enduring debate about Christmas in the US. Both of these debates brand a nation as being linked to a specific religious tradition, while implicitly creating a hierarchy that places other religions below. This essentializing of belief or of "otherness" often leads to political results. Think, for example, of the attempts of the political Right in this country to turn Obama into a Muslim. Are they saying that a Muslim should not be president regardless of his or her qualifications? Or think of the attempts of the French government—for even enlightened France can descend into this type of behavior—to expel the Roma from Paris.

Indeed, for better or worse, we cannot think of that which we call history, culture, the lives of nations, or the lives of individuals without some reference to religion. Even those like me, who have grown to have a rather vehement dislike for what I perceive as religion's nefarious influence on the course of history, cannot do without frequently engaging religion, or, as mentioned earlier, being touched by its spell. As Clifford Geertz argued long ago (borrowing from Max Weber) in a rightly famous essay, we live, and are caught, in unavoidable "webs of significance."[1] These cultural webs bind us to specific religious forms. Although we may understand other religions and cultures, our diverse visions of the world and of ourselves are deeply imbedded in the religious culture into which we were born and in the things we were taught and learned as children and as adults. In a rather Buñuelesque fashion—Luis Buñuel was extremely anti-clerical but could not stop directing films about religion—I, and many others like me, while professing a total absence of religion, think, act, and are trapped as well in webs of significance that are spun by religion.

---

[1] Clifford Geertz, *The Interpretations of Culture: Selected Essays* (New York: Basic Books, 1973) chapter 1.

Of course, one ought to state the obvious before proceeding to other themes: absence of religion or a belief in god does not mean an absence of what is called morality, spirituality, or ethics. One of the most annoying things about discussing these matters is the rather shortsighted view that religion is necessary to be a "moral" person or to behave ethically, a position that often prompts a running argument with my students. It is true that most religions provide a ready-made code of conduct—not that I approve of those codes or of their systems of rewards and punishments. They also provide, certainly the religions of the Book do, heavens or hells to encourage compliance. On this point there is little I could add to what has already been articulated by Plato. In the *Republic*, he argued persuasively for a life in which men and women would behave ethically and seek the good not because of any rewards or punishments in the afterlife, but because to do evil to others is to harm oneself first and foremost. I admit that "good" and "evil," "ethical" and "unethical" are highly contested concepts. And Plato, at the end of the *Republic* let us down badly by introducing the myth of Er as yet another mysterious incentive—transmigration of souls, rewards in heaven, and a whole array of Pythagorean mysteries—to right behavior.

Escaping the Terror of History

By now, you will be ready to ask: what does all of this have to do with the terror of history and the uses of religion as a means of denying history's burdens? Simply put, I do not wish to deny religion's historical reality, nor its central role in human history. While I wish to re-emphasize that this is a discussion about religion and not about god or the gods, I also wish to make a further point. There are crises along the long road of human existence that provoke either overwhelming stress or almost unbearable disruptions. Individuals and groups, unable to cope with what seem terrible forces gathering against them or suffering from a deep sense of alienation and despair, seek to escape these conditions or to deny their historicity. Think, for example, of the Holocaust. Many have argued (though few scholars do so anymore) that it was a unique event, not comparable to other excesses against humanity and, thus, outside history. Although I do not agree with the idea that there are events outside history (but feel rather that events such as the Holocaust should be historicized as a lesson to posterity), the important thing here is that there are some who would deny the historicity of the event—a cruelty after all perpetrated by men and women against other men and women—and argue that the Shoah was an incomprehensible divine act, not to be fully grasped by the human intellect. The history of the Shoah is so utterly horrendous that there is always the temptation to exclude it from human actions and to think that such deeds are not inherent in human agency. I fear that they are.[2]

Several questions need to be answered. What mechanisms or events trigger an escape from history? How do certain forms of religious experiences, both individual and communal, permit us to deny historical reality? Or how, in a certain sense, can one construct an alternate plane of existence that may appear at first glance to be better than the life one leads and that, most of all, may allow a person or a group to escape from the terrifying occurrences and patterns of human history? Large catastrophes could trigger these reactions, either

---

[2] See the series published by Princeton University Press, "Human Rights and Crimes Against Humanity" (four volumes have been published so far), which explores some of the most horrific violence against humans by other humans.

partially or fully. Yet, not all plagues, natural disasters, or manmade crises lead to such responses. Outcomes and responses depend, to a large extent, on historical contexts, on the presence or absence of charismatic leadership, on the level of understanding or misunderstanding of specific populations as to the nature of the crisis.

Catastrophes are of course not the only cause for a turning away from history. Gradual, abrupt, and above all drastic social and economic changes can have either a cumulative or immediate impact on large segments of the population. The dramatic social, economic, and religious transformations that marked the transition from late medieval times to the early modern unleashed millenarian agitations such as that of the German peasant uprising of 1525 and a whole host of local and regional apocalyptic movements that announced to their respective followers the end of history and time. A different form of response was the witch craze that swept Western Europe between the very late fifteenth century and the mid-seventeenth centuries. It resulted in the systematic execution of thousands of people, mostly old women. Although the witch craze was a historical phenomenon with a clearly defined trajectory, causes, and outcomes, the ideological depiction of witch beliefs by those on top as a reason for persecution provided an alternative to the other well-known great early modern Western narratives: science, discovery, centralized monarchical authority, and the emergence of the state. In a very real sense, all these elements (the harbingers of modernity) which should have, in theory, moved Western societies towards a more rational and enlightened view of the world (as they did in the eighteenth century), paradoxically fanned the fires of persecution, misogyny, and scapegoating. Below, we will revisit these topics, but it is important to note how the conflation of new technologies of knowledge and religion led to untold horror and desperate attempts to escape history.

Before proceeding to the examples, I do not wish to leave the reader with the impression, an impression prompted perhaps by my comments in the previous pages, that history moves from irrational to rational and back again in some form of linear progression. I do not know whether the Enlightenment was the highest point of Western history; nor that progress, if by that we mean material progress and technological change, is the criteria by which we should measure human achievements. To paraphrase Nietzsche, it is about values. It is not by calculating the increase in material wealth or technology that we should measure progress, but by what our values are, and by our constant readiness to reevaluate those values. Clearly, in terms of our desire to respect the lives of others, their freedom, and culture, we have failed miserably.

The Greeks, who were perhaps the first humans to gaze unflinchingly into the heart of darkness and who understood, or at least some of them did, the meaninglessness and emptiness of the universe, pulled back from irrationality, as tempting as it was, by building an elaborate edifice of rationality and restraint. "Know thyself" and "nothing in excess" became the ideal ruling principles of their lives. As worthy as these maxims are, they only reveal their opposites: that human life is often about excesses, and that very seldom do we know ourselves. Having written this, allow me to make a small point and complicate things further: the ideals of the Enlightenment and the belief of Enlightenment philosophers in progress only obscured and veiled the underlying irrationality and chaos of most European lives.

But enough of this, we should turn to actual responses or attempts, usually failed, to confront the excesses of history, the swift passing of time, and the permanent and edgy irrationality of our individual and collective lives. Responses are not always necessarily those of groups. Often people confront the specific Scylla and Charybdis of their individual lives through religion and other practices. We seek to make rational or, at least, somewhat understandable, overwhelming historical events as well as the less obvious but nonetheless always menacing disruptions of historical change. Some mystical or meditative states represent a clear turning away from historical reality and lead to the embracing of alternative forms of existence and awareness of time. In the most emphatic fashion, most great mystics and religious figures have argued for their direct and intimate relationship with god (or the gods), a way of thinking about the world that flies in the face of history or reality, as understood by many. Think, for example, of the life of St. Francis of Assisi. He was certainly one of the most, if not the most, influential late medieval mystic. His life inspired many; his teachings led to millennial agitation and radical social and theological (one may describe some of the views held by some of Francis' followers as heterodox) forms of religious practices. Such was his influence that almost eight hundred years later, I was, as an adolescent, taken by Francis' example, and most of my students, who are assigned *The Little Flowers of St. Francis* as one of the texts they must read in my course on mysticism, are always quite moved by what seems to them his genuine renunciation of material wealth and embracing of poverty.

Francis of Assisi

Francis (c. 1182–1226) was born into a world in which social and economic structures were changing rapidly. Trade and a money economy were transforming social relations, fueling a wave of urbanization in Western Europe in general and in Italy in particular. The bourgeoisie accumulated wealth while eagerly yearning for salvation. This inherent contradiction created a conundrum for most enterprising middling sorts. Under the impetus of new economic realities, new forms of spirituality and novel attitudes towards property and wealth swept the West. Francis' eventual message emerged from these contexts, but his preaching, shortly after the beginning of his mission, was not new. Before Francis, Peter Waldo (or Valdes) and his followers had articulated a powerful critique of these new economic forms and of the Church's wealth. Branded as heterodox, the Waldensians faced mounting resistance and persecution, as did the Cathars, whose heresy was widespread in late-twelfth-century southern France.

The son of a merchant and born in Assisi (Umbria) around 1182, Francis grew up not very differently from his youthful companions. He was, as were many of his generation and station in life, deeply influenced by courtly romances, dreams of courageous martial deeds, and other such fantasies. Having read an idealized life of Francis early in my adolescence, I, almost fifty years afterwards, acknowledge honestly (and once again) to what an extent my own life and political views were shaped by Francis' seemingly radical message. As has become a trope in the lives of saints, poets, and other sensitive people—think of Ignatius of Loyola or the young men of the Lost Generation—the experience of war (against nearby Perugia) and of being wounded deeply transformed Francis into a reflective and introspective young man. From this awakening, a radical transformation indeed, he rejected material things and embraced voluntary poverty and a life of preaching. His life, both as the subject of learned studies and hagiographical accounts, is well known.[3] His preaching to the animals, his special sensitivity to nature, the centrality of apostolic poverty in his preaching, and his emphasis on Christ's humanity signaled new possibilities for Christianity. His reception of the stigmata at Mount La Verne shortly before his death in 1226 marked a significant moment in Western history and spirituality. If Jesus was, according to Christian theology, both within history and outside it, Francis, by physically reliving Jesus' passion, also stood within and outside history and time. Never mind that his own order, the Franciscans, rejected the core of Francis' message and emphasized the importance of monastic establishments (thus property), education, and teaching against Francis' firm rejection of any compromise with the world of property and owning things. Although Francis failed to convince some of his closest followers, others heard his ringing message. Never mind that he never challenged the authority of the Church or deviated from orthodoxy. Never mind that his emphasis on voluntary poverty led to, unintentionally for sure, a sharp distinction between those who had wealth and gave it up for the love of Christ and those who had the misfortune to be born and live in poverty not out of choice, robbing the latter finally of their standing in Christian society. But what did Francis' life and preaching mean to his contemporaries, and how does his life play into our story?

The question here is not whether his heroic deeds, frequent mystical raptures, and his final reception of the stigmata —described in rhapsodic details by the mildly subversive *Little Flowers of St. Francis* (written many years after Francis' death)—were "real" or not. For most of Francis' contempo-

---

[3] On the life of Francis, see Jacques Le Goff, *Saint François d'Assise* (Paris: Gallimard, 1999) and *The Little Flowers of St. Francis*, ed. Raphael Brown (New York: Image Books/Doubleday, 1991).

raries and for those living even centuries afterwards, the stories told and retold about him had an unimpeachable reality. In early thirteenth-century Europe, a world in which social, economic, and cultural transformations and changes in Church doctrine (most notably at the Fourth Lateran Council [1215]) created growing anxieties, St. Francis' deeds and example offered solace and important lessons as well about living a true apostolic life. Historians, such as R. I. Moore and others, have focused on the early decades of the thirteenth century as marking the genesis of what has been described as "persecuting societies."[4] Although there is considerable historiographical discussion about whether the period truly marked the beginning of harsher attitudes towards heretics, Jews, Muslims, and others, it is fairly clear that wholesale changes were in the making. These changes, at the same time, deeply affected the spiritual life of Christians throughout the medieval West.

Beyond embellishing what I have already stated in previous paragraphs, one should note that Francis' actions generated two different types of alternatives. First, at a personal level, Francis' conversion or awakening, ascetic practices, and life of preaching brought him out of his own milieu and freed him from daily concerns, that is, took him out, as it were, from a set of social historical constraints. In many respects, some of the most charming passages detailing Francis' adventures are those that reflect an element of random choice, of "playing the game" by none of the acceptable rules, or doing so by completely new rules. In reaching a bifurcation on the road and not knowing which direction to choose,

[4] R. I. Moore, *The Formation of a Persecuting Society: Authority and Deviance in Western Europe, 950–1250*, 2nd ed. (Malden, MA: Blackwell Publishing, 2007); and Carlo Ginzburg, *Ecstasies: Deciphering the Witches' Sabbath*, trans. Raymond Rosenthal (New York: Pantheon Books, 1991).

Francis asked one of his followers to swirl wildly and whatever road he faced at the end of his dance, that unknown road they would follow. I write this with a bit of envy, as I, and I am sure many others, presently lead lives in which we strain hopelessly to leave nothing to chance. This is even more ironic since we know that plans are easily overthrown by fate, chance, luck, illness, howsoever we wish to describe those fateful instances that overturn our best-laid plans for a well-ordered and predictable life.

Francis' story recalls some of the 1960s attitudes towards life: the absence of planning, the lack of concern about the near or far future, the exquisite enjoyment of the moment, the rejection of the material world, and with it and only in a limited sense, a rejection of history and time. Francis had an immense impact on his contemporaries, as communes and the so-called hippies did on the culture of the 1960s. When faced with rapid change and uncertain times, Francis, like young people in the sixties (of whom I was one), escaped the burdens and terror of history through mystical visions, the embracing of poverty, and an apostolic life. As was the case in the 1960s, many in our society, often coming from a social background not unlike that of Francis, joined communes, moved to the sound of new and intoxicating music, rejected material gains, joined the peace movement (which was deeply historical), and, when finally everything failed, took to mind-bending, drug-induced escape, a kind of chemical substitute for religious mysticism.

Confronted with the angst of everyday life, with the boredom of the quotidian, with the absurdities and cruelties of history (endless warfare and communal strife in Italy during Francis' life, the Vietnam war in the 1960s and the newly gained awareness of the burdens of racial discrimination), individuals and small groups turned their backs on their societies' expectations and chose different paths that set them sometimes at odds with their parents and peers and placed them outside normative historical processes. Some, such as Francis, we canonize, even as we are very careful to reject or neglect his example and message. Others, such as the young women and men who gave life to the sixties, we idealize or vilify according to our political bent; yet, we borrow their music, their fashions, and their poetry, while consciously following other paths that lead to careers, families, and compromise.

How very enticing and powerful these examples remain. How moving it must have been for those who met Francis or heard stories about him. Similarly, many lived vicariously through the deeds of others in the 1960s. It is said that if all those who claim to have attended the great concert at Woodstock had really been there, the attendance would have numbered in the millions. For Woodstock was that unique combination of music, peace, and non-violence (or at least was idealized as such) that even for those who were not fortunate enough to be there—and I was not there—represented an alternative to war and the corporate world, and a slim possibility to dehistoricize our lives. Rereading this now, past the fortieth anniversary of Woodstock, I am amazed at how those glorious days of music and mud still resonate even in our apathetic age.

Individuals and communities do not require a plague like the one that vanquished many in 1348–50 or a September 11th to loosen our ties to history. We are always, somewhat unconsciously, attempting to escape history, the burdens of fleeting time, and their inexorable terrors and ever changing landscapes. Francis did, as did numerous other medieval mystics (whether orthodox or heterodox), first by entering into a rich interior spiritual life and then by articulating his visions to a wider world. So did many young people in the sixties who, while not sharing any particular or formal religion, had, at least for a short while, as much spirituality and as great a sense of citizenship in a benign universe as did any medieval mystic.

Second, Francis' life and example had other consequences that propelled many of his later followers against history. He was widely seen as the second coming of Christ, and consequently his life and message served as a rallying point and inspiration for a groundswell of millenarian expectations that swept parts of Western Europe in the 1260s and, in a more diminished form, in the early fourteenth century. The end of the world, by which was meant the end of time and history, was anxiously expected in 1266, with Francis as the harbinger of the Second Coming and the final wars. These apocalyptic ideas, which had long been part and parcel of Western history and which, according to Norman Cohn had their origins in ancient Mesopotamian and Zoroastrian beliefs, have had a remarkable vitality in Western culture.[5] Their blossoming in times of change, uncertainty, and catastrophes is a telling sign of our enduring discomfort with historical processes. These millenarian outbursts punctuate our history. In the 1260s, bands of flagellants took to the road; their self-inflicted punishment was a form of purgation of their own perceived excesses and of the evilness of the world. It was a powerful attempt to return humanity and the world to god. The Church, which was of course an institution deeply

---

[5] On these topics, see the two very important books by Norman Cohn, *Cosmos, Chaos, and the World to Come: The Ancient Roots of Apocalyptic Faith*, 2nd ed. (New Haven, CT: Yale University Press, 2001); and his *The Pursuit of the Millennium: Revolutionary Millenarians and Mystical Anarchists of the Middle Ages*, rev. ed. (New York: Oxford University Press, 1970).

grounded in history, did not look with pleasure on these activities, condemning the flagellants as heretical and uncanonical. It would do so again in 1348 when, in the wake of the Black Death, flagellants reappeared throughout the West.

Francis' impact was not just limited to widespread expectations for the end of the world and time or to the flagellants' peculiar religiosity. Francis' radical followers remained for decades after his death in what can be described as an almost permanent state of subversion and resistance in expectation of the end of time. They did so into the late thirteenth and early fourteenth centuries, that is, for almost a century after Francis' death. These Fraticelli or little brothers, as they were known, became radical proponents of poverty and of an evangelical Christianity that was, in the eyes of the Church, deeply intertwined with heresy, prophesy, and enduring expectations of dramatic changes within the Church. We meet some of these characters, vividly drawn, in Umberto Eco's *The Name of the Rose,* but they had far more real counterparts. The idea of an Angelical Pope who would usher in the Last Days and the end of history was fanned by Celestine V's election to, and shortly thereafter by his famous resignation from, the papal throne in 1294, as well as by the coming of a new century. These ideas, circulating widely throughout the West, were part of complex set of traditional and, at the same time, revolutionary ideas that lingered in parts of Italy, mostly Calabria, into the early modern period. We find echoes of these beliefs in the life, deeds, and writings of someone like Tommaso Campanella, fairly well known for his defense of Galileo, but less known for his long prison term in Spanish custody for plotting and writings about a universal monarchy (first Spain and later France) that would bring final peace to earth. He also authored the enchanting utopian work, *The City of the Sun*, a work in which Christianity and property played no role.[6]

Escaping History and Time through Religion

The historical record allows for the writing of a parallel history of Christianity, as Jeffrey Burton Russell did more than three decades ago, that would provide a linear description of the tensions between orthodox beliefs on the one hand—as enunciated by those in control—and prophetic, heretical, or millenarian movements.[7] The well-informed reader knows the high (or low depending on one's views) points along this trajectory. There was the great peasant uprising in England in 1381, which, although having solid social and economic roots, had also a strong religious and egalitarian base. Then followed the Hussite rebellion that agitated most of Central Europe in the late fifteenth century, and about a century later the German peasant uprising of 1525. Thomas Müntzer's radical Biblicism combined with an ahistorical millenarian fervor led to a series of utopian experiments of which sixteenth-century Münster is only the best-known example.[8] Nonetheless, we would be in peril here to think—because of my examples and chronological bent—that escaping history is a purely Christian phenomenon, limited to discreet chronological periods.

In reality, these phenomena are, of course, not limited to Christianity, to the West, or to specific chronological periods.

[6] On Campanella, see Tommaso Campanella, *La città del sole: dialogo poetico / The City of the Sun: A Poetical Dialogue*, trans. and introduction by Daniel J. Donno (Berkeley, CA: University of California Press, 1981).
[7] Jeffrey Burton Russell, *A History of Medieval Christianity: Prophecy & Order* (Arlington Heights, IL: H. Davidson, originally published in 1968, reprint in 1986).
[8] See Cohn, *The Pursuit of the Millennium*.

In a very broad sense, some forms of religious observance in the ancient world belong into a category one may correctly describe as against, or attempts to escape, history and time. The classical world's pessimistic bent, so obviously present in the widespread belief in astrology, contrasts vividly with the orgiastic celebrations of the cult of Dionysus with its so-called Bacchic excesses. Many ascetic tendencies, already discernable in Plato and other classical-age philosophers, came to the forefront in the second century CE, around the same time that Christianity began to make inroads among the population of the Roman Empire. Neoplatonism, above all in Plotinus' work, turned philosophy into religion and, together with a whole collection of mystery religions—Hermeticism, the cult of Demeter at Eleusis, the cults of Isis, Mithras, and other such redemptive religious forms (among them Christianity) made a bid for the allegiance of either the masses or small elite groups of neophytes, depending on the nature of outreach of each of these sects.

Marguerite Yourcenar's impressive and moving fictional biography of the emperor Hadrian quoted Flaubert to the effect that, while Hadrian ruled (117–38 CE), the gods were dead, and Christianity had not yet come fully to the fore. Men stood alone. Hadrian, an enlightened despot, may have been able to stand without gods or religion, but most of his subjects were not. This is why, as the empire declined in the shadows of military dictatorship (regardless of how enlightened that dictatorship was) and its inhabitants experienced growing social and economic malaise, the majority of the people escaped the pervasive gloom of their world by embracing redemptive religions that promised a better life and salvation (whatever that meant) in the world beyond. Astrology after all tells you that your fate is already written in the stars. The cults of Isis, Demeter, Mithras, and of the Christ tell you that redemption awaits you after death. Gibbon's celebrated description of the second century as the most peaceful age that mankind has ever known may be true in terms of the absence of warfare (though Rome's borders were not that peaceful), but it was a peace bought at the price of great despair. It ushered in an awful revolution, the effects of which we are still suffering today. Asceticism, the sharp separation of soul (or mind) and body, the perception of the body as a prison from which the soul needs to be freed by constant fasting, sexual abstinence, and other such extreme measures easily identifiable with new religious forms emerging in the West were some of the results of that sweeping cultural transformation that I have described as an awful revolution. These trends, denying the body and embracing systems of belief that led to a transcendent awareness of god or the gods became the propelling forces behind the emergence of monasticism and the writings of the Church Fathers, most of all, those of the great St. Augustine of Hippo. In turn, these novel institutions and religious discourses shaped, and still shape, the mentality of the West.

What else but an escape from history is the Late Antique deeply felt sense, as articulated by some religious figures, that living in the world, in the City of Man as constituted under a waning Rome, was not worth the effort. That one's true homeland was located in heaven and that death itself was nothing but a release from the temptations and oppressions of daily life. Barbarian invasions, civil wars, deteriorating economies, the growing bondage of peasants to the soil, and other such pleasantries only confirmed the inclination to deny the world, its history, and the swift changes occurring in a dying Roman Empire. Although historically Christianity, the religion that emerged triumphant in the end from the bevy of competing redemptive religions, did assume a leading

58

role in the affairs of the world, preserving Roman structures and attempting to create a semblance of continuity and order, this should not lead us to ignore the fact that the new cults, of which Christianity was one, with their mysteries, emphasis on faith, and redemptive messages, had a signal role in demolishing a civic culture that had provided a civilizing context for life throughout the Mediterranean world. One may ask: how did Christianity and other mystery religions help wreck the civilizations that had flourished in Greece and Rome for more than seven centuries? Although other social and economic factors played a part, the emphasis of the new religions, and Christianity most of all, on the afterlife instead of the here-and-now and on the superiority of belief over reason, as well as their strong condemnation of classical plays, classical art, and entertainment, and the idea that power came from god or the gods and not from human institutions sounded the death knell for the world of classical antiquity.

Although I have focused on the Mediterranean world and the origins of Christianity, every age and place has witnessed similar individual and/or communal beliefs and actions that, although historical phenomena in themselves, represent a rejection of history and attempts to step out of historical processes, to escape the crushing reality of everyday expectations, of the dark components of historical development. It is the wildness and unpredictability of these attempts to flee history, their open-ended quality, their illusory hopes that make them so relevant and worthy of notice. Ranging from religiously inspired desires to become one with god—through mystical rapture, meditation, or ascetic practices—to the wish to erase social distinctions and to create or recreate a paradise in the here-and-now, or to leave the world altogether—as in apocalyptic movements or social upheavals, these responses to either social and economic change or unusual events are tell-tale signs of our discomfort with the world as we have found it, with the world as is.

Although the locus of my reflections is mostly the Judeo-Christian West, it is clear that the religions of the Book, and that includes Islam as well, do not have a monopoly on these types of responses. Indian sadhus or sanyasis (those who re-nounce sexuality and the world to gain a higher level of spiri-tuality and freedom from the wheel of life and reincarnation) —some of the world's greatest religious movements were born on the banks of the Ganges River—shared in this universal desire to either radically transform history or to reject it. The ancient world, the civilization that invented history itself as a form of knowledge—Herodotus, Thucydides, and the great Roman historians are the best example of this creation of a discipline—contained within itself these tensions, as we have seen previously.

One can look at this problem however from a different perspective. One may argue that escaping history and the grip of time is a natural part of the ebb and flow of history itself. Tensions are part of a complex dialectical process that propels history and us into the future. Or we can easily re-duce all these movements to sets of social and economic ex-planations. Religion, even if understood as one of the prod-ucts of historical forces, is always a troublesome category. And it is precisely its troubled status and the elusive nature of belief that makes religion-borne escapes from history so per-tinent to this story. After all, to the true believer explanations are unnecessary. We may find it almost incomprehensible that in the late twentieth century, well-educated young men and women in suburban San Diego truly believed that, after committing suicide, they would be transported into a higher plane of existence and bodily lifted to a spaceship—a story told already earlier in this chapter—but these young men and women found such an assertion wholly rational and believable. We may shudder and be horrified that nineteen young men, many of them highly educated and from fairly well-to-do families, purposely crashed planes, passengers, and themselves into buildings, killing thousands in the process. Such acts are always done in the name of high religiously inflicted political ideals and a deeply felt personal sense of martyrdom and redemption.

The troublesome thing is that September 11, 2001, was only unusual because of the targets chosen and the spectacular use of technology. Similar deeds have been carried out throughout history and are still being carried out throughout the world. History, as written, experienced, and plotted in the West, runs counter to how the past, present, and future are imagined elsewhere. But within the Western tradition, history itself has been, and continues to be, rejected. Westerners are not ignorant of suicidal acts of martyrdom, or of acts of violence that result in the deaths of many. What I am saying here, once again in repetitive fashion, is that the unfolding of historical events contains within it the kernel for resistance. And that, at the same time, the most common individual and communal form of resistance to, or rejection of the suffocating grip of history is through some form of religious experience, either mystic rapture or communal feeling translated into millennial dreams or utopian fantasies.

The enduring frequency of these religious movements—even in our postmodern world—alerts us to their significance. In many ways, communities of believers stand apart from and outside of social and political norms. Often such beliefs lead to a rejection of the constraints and authority of the state. When English puritanical radicals in the seventeenth century or John Ashcroft, the former head of the Justice Department under George W. Bush, proclaimed that they had no king but Jesus, they voiced sentiments that went directly to the heart of the matter at issue here. That is, that when confronted with unjust and oppressive rulers, as was the case in seventeenth-century England, devotees of religious movements reject the situation in the name of god, join the ranks of the godly, as peasants did in Germany in 1525, and take up arms against (and kill) the ungodly.

Escapes from history are often violent events, and they can lead to great bloodshed. The downtrodden and oppressed have always found in religion a solace for their plight, even though other forms of escape were always available, and even though some would argue that religion was after all a way of perpetuating and legitimizing oppression. Religion also provides a powerful vehicle for escape and the possibility to transform historical processes. That escape is usually a violent one. I am, of course, not saying anything new here. As noted earlier in citing Housley, most violence in the Western world and elsewhere has religious roots. But I am far less interested in the violence that emerges from the confrontation between opposing views about orthodoxy, as for example the religious wars that plagued Europe in the wake of the Reformation, than I am in the violence generated by dire social conditions, leading often to apocalyptic outbursts. These are precisely the communal movements that wish to erase history, to usher in Christ's second coming in the case of Christianity or the Messiah in the case of Judaism and, thus, the end of time.

The End of Time

An excellent example of this phenomenon in Judaism is the millennial agitation focused on the enigmatic figure of Sabbatai Zevi (1621–1676) that swept Jewish communities in the early seventeenth century. This movement, centered around the figure of a false Messiah—of which there are still echoes today and which is replicated among some Lubavitchers in their belief that their beloved rabbi is soon to be resurrected —shows how religious fervor and the expectations of the coming of the Messiah could unleash extraordinary historical events. While highly historical, their aim was always the end of history itself. Many Jews throughout Europe sold their goods, their houses, and poured into northern European and Mediterranean ports, seeking passage to Palestine. They sought to witness, and to be part of, the coming of the Messiah, the restoration of Israel, and its final triumph over the godless gentiles. The religious fervor was not confined to the Sephardic diaspora, finding support among the Ashkenazim as well. Glückel of Hameln (1646–1724) tells us in her memoirs that her father-in-law sold his property and made ready to travel from Hamburg to Palestine so as to be among those at the final revelation of the Messiah. Even after Sabbatai Zevi's conversion to Islam under pressure from the agents of the Sublime Port, the millenarian expectations remained.[9]

One can spend a lifetime exploring the social and economic contexts in which these phenomena took, and continue to take place. In the case of Sabbatai Zevi, the growing restraints on Jewish life, the memories of exile from Spain, and other factors triggered the rise of Sabbatianism. Other contexts yielded different responses, though the aim of escaping from normative history or, in the case of Jews, from someone else's history, remained the same. Some of the stories collected by Martin Buber, a noted philosopher and mystic

---

[9] Gershom Scholem, *Sabbatai Sevi: The Mystical Messiah, 1626–1676*, trans. R. J. Zwi Werblowsky (Princeton, NJ: Princeton University Press, 1973).

twentieth-century German Jew, about the Baal Shem Tov (1698–1760 and the most influential of all Hassidic rabbis) and the early Hassidic masters have, in their simplicity and religious joys, a great resemblance to the accounts of early Franciscans, their deeds, and their rejection of established rules and social hierarchies.

Fear

Fear also underlined most of these forms of escape. Mircea Eliade in a rightly famous essay already mentioned in the introduction to this book describes the terror of primitive men and women as they waited out the night, surrounded by menacing predators and uncertainty.[10] Throughout history, we have worked very hard to lessen or eliminate some of our most basic fears. Obviously, most of us do not fear that predatory animals will invade our houses or apartments in the middle of the night, or, at least, not those with four legs. Nor do we fear today throughout most of the Western world the possibility of dying of hunger or the scourge of witches. Instead, other fears have emerged to undermine our sense of security and to disturb our equilibrium. Against the fear of war, the fear of losing our social and economic standing, or living too long in loneliness and decrepitude, we build, though not often successfully, many barriers to protect us and to keep the new terrors at bay.

My arguments here reprise those of Freud in the opening pages of his *Civilization and Its Discontents* to the effect that while technology and progress have advanced the quality of our lives in some fashion or another, they have also diminished that quality by creating new anxieties and fears. In the

---

[10] Mircea Eliade, *Cosmos and History: The Myth of the Eternal Return* , trans. Willard R. Trask (New York: Harper, 1959). See chapter entitled "The Terror of History."

West, as well as in other parts of the world, one may find numerous examples of how collective fears emerge, are managed by those in power, and often given a religious or semi-religious veneer as a way to provide the many with a form of release or escape. Jean Delaumeau's brilliant book, *La peur en Occident* (*Fear in the West*), long ago pointed to the special circumstances generated by the transition from medieval to early modern, the widespread fear of social, economic, and political transformations. It was not difficult, he argued, to focus these social fears into well-defined and easily understood channels. The European "witch craze" or "witch hunt" that swept most of Western Europe from the late fifteenth century to the 1670s or so is but one of our best examples of how very rational, powerful, and well educated people can construct a complex edifice of beliefs. That in the West those accused of, and condemned for, practicing witchcraft were mostly women, old, and socially and economically inferior to their accusers gives us a sense of the social forces at work, of the making of scapegoats and the like. Yet, there was something deeper in meaning in the tragic story of the witch hunt and in its sorry outcome.

In a time of dramatic social and economic transformations, punctuated by the formation of more centralized monarchies, religious fracture, sectarian wars, and new scientific knowledge and discoveries, the fear of these changes prompted a religious response. The emergence of Satan as the focus for witch beliefs and the widely held idea that witchcraft was an alternative religion led to public and popular-supported witch burnings and hangings. If one could just get rid of these horrid witches, then everything would be all right. It sounds, and it was, a bit irrational, but how much more irrational was the fear of witches than our modern fears of terrorism, weapons of mass destruction (even if non-existent), and other such modern ways of channeling modern anxieties? For most people it is much better to worry about such matters than about real and depressing facts, such as the erosion of civil liberties, the deteriorating environment, economic malaise, and the growing distance between social classes. Blame it on the witches or, as some modern politicians or fundamentalist have done, blame it on Bin Laden and/or homosexuals.

The Witch Craze

The witch craze is one of those historical phenomena that requires a close look. It was a great deal about power and the transition of the West to modernity. It was also one of the high points in Western misogyny. Paradoxically, it occurred in the midst of one of the most exciting intellectual periods in Western history. And this is a grim reminder that we always walk a perilous path and that the tilting point between reason and irrationality is a narrow one. Some of the most learned men in Western Europe, Newton among them, accepted the reality of witchcraft and the validity of witch confessions with all the absurdities that such statements, garnered through torture or suggestive and insistent questioning, produced. Those accused of witchcraft often confessed to mischief, worshiping the devil, and gathering at nocturnal ceremonies for the witches' Sabbath. At these gathering, or so the confessions and the accusations went, they engaged in blasphemous recreations of the Mass, sexual orgies, lewd dancing, child sacrifices, and even cannibalism. Art, from Dürer to Goya, depicted this dark and ominous world of witches. That these confessions had an eerie similarity should not surprise us, since the questions, pounded again and again into mostly uneducated and frightened old and vulnerable women, provided clear guidelines as to the appropriate and expected answers and confessions.

That the European witch craze was contemporary with the Renaissance, the Scientific Revolution, the Reformation, the rise of centralized monarchies, and other markers of "modernity," alerts us to the danger of times when rapid change is in the air. In the midst of these dramatic transformations and horrific sectarian struggles, some—St. Teresa of Avila, John of the Cross, Pascal, and others—went on mystical journeys into the self, ineffable interior pilgrimages that shut out the world, history, and time. Others joined the innumerable millenarian and popular risings that agitated Western Europe in the sixteenth and seventeenth centuries: from Sebastianism (the hope that king Sebastián of Portugal, lost in the North African battlefield at Alcazar Quibir in 1578, would return to lead his realm and all of Christianity into the end of history) to the redemptive messianic liberation of Israel promised by Sabbatai Zevi. And yet others embraced mysterious and esoteric forms of knowledge such as magic, alchemy, astrology, and hermeticism. None of these forms of escape was as popular as the belief in witches.

Most people in Western Europe (with some notable individual and geographical exceptions, Spain among them) accepted the existence of witches. Since in the religions of the Book, to believe in God is, ipso facto, to believe in the devil, this almost dualistic doctrine, reinforced by the long-lasting impact that Manichaeism has had on Western thought, provided a handy excuse for the cruelties of life and for the awful historical events befalling most of Europe. Blame it on the witches! To believe in witches from the late fifteenth century to the second half of the seventeenth century was perfectly rational. To do so afterward was irrational indeed, and a proof of ignorance. In that crucial century and a half, the belief that Satan manipulated history and that one could return to normalcy by a wholesale slaughtering of those accused and convicted of witchcraft offered a ready solution to the anxieties of the times. Unlike the processions and pious ceremonies prompted by the plague, or even the flagellants, who after all did mostly damage only to themselves, the witch craze affected thousands of lives and left a legacy of persecution that has endured in the West into our own lifetimes.

I am of course not arguing that witchcraft itself, or what the West calls or identifies as witchcraft, is a clear form of escape from history. What the West calls witchcraft can be identified in religious contexts in other parts of the world. Certainly as practiced elsewhere or, as Carlo Ginzburg showed magisterially in his study of the *Benandanti,* as the archaic survival of agricultural cults, these observances have had a rich life outside Christianity's rigid dichotomy between good and evil, between god and Satan. Having grown up in Cuba and having visited Brazil several times, I have always been —and this is odd since, as I have said before, I always think of myself as either an agnostic or a devout atheist—surprised and moved by the cadence and rituals of Cuban *Santería* and Brazilian *Candomblé,* both of them, not unlike Haitian voodoo, widespread systems of beliefs that conflate African religious forms and devotion to the *orixas* (or African gods) with Christian devotion of the saints. Here is where the certainty of Western orthodoxy comes face to face with the challenge of mysteries. These mysteries, not unlike the belief in witches or the persecution of witches, represent a not-so-veiled attempt to escape history's grip. But to return to Cuba, growing up there, I was deeply marked—even if I must admit that the enervating music and alcohol played a significant role—by a particular *Santería* ceremony on the eve of Santa

Barbara and by the visions that half century ago came to me after midnight on December 4th, 1957, the feast day of Santa Barbara or, for *Santería*, the feast day of Chango, an African *orixa*. In many respects, those visions shaped my life even after I left my faith behind. (See chapter 3.)

Many years afterward, while visiting Salvador, the magical capital of the state of Bahía in Brazil, I was fortunate enough to attend a *Candomblé* ceremony in the outskirts of the city. For several hours the chants and responses in Yoruba (a West African language), the music, and dancing went on until at a specific moment in the long ceremony, the *orixas*, the African deities, according to the participants, descended and took hold of some of the dancers. Changing their costumes to garments that identified them as specific gods and goddesses, they now chanted and danced among the people. It was an overwhelming experience at a personal and emotional level. As a historian, I thought that this is precisely what Bacchic excesses (a form of religious experience) must have been like, a moment in time and out of time in which, caught in the frenzy of music and drink, one steps out of the bounds of reason and time, out of history and its terror. The performers, catching many of those in attendance in their wake, carried them into another plane of experience and existence. This is also what Christian missionaries had long branded as witchcraft.

Certain folk beliefs and practices in Europe, Cuba, Brazil, and elsewhere in the world identified by learned missionaries and mendicant preachers, described in erudite treatises, and the target of legal codes, papal bulls, and persecution came to be identified as witchcraft. That certainly was the case in Europe at the end of the Middle Ages, and the consequence, as we have already seen, was the persecution of mostly old woman and their cruel fate. The reality, as shown recently by historians and anthropologists, was very different indeed. My argument here is, once again, not that witchcraft was a well-defined escape from history, although some forms of Satanism may have been. The argument is that the witch craze itself, generated from the upper echelons of society and sponsored by governments and churches (Protestant and Catholic alike), dramatically adorned with the theatricality of public burnings, and enjoying overwhelming popular support, was in itself either one of the most malevolent conspiracies by those on top (seeking to focus attention on vulnerable and helpless victims), or else it was a flight from history.

By overturning reason in the name of reason, by creating a whole mythology of demons, witches, and mischief—all of it spicily dressed up with sexual and violent motifs—those on top found a space in which, stepping out of normal history, they embraced a world of myth, darkness, and make-believe. Perhaps the remarkable thing about the witch craze is how those on top could operate so comfortably on such two contradictory intellectual levels. Noted scientists, philosophers, statesmen, and church dignitaries carried our their research and duties without missing a beat, while, with no apparent disjunction, they wrote learned treatises about witchcraft, presided over trials, and were complicit in the torture and execution visited upon those accused and convicted of witchcraft. Of course, such a disconnect is not unusual, and our own age has witnessed inexplicable atrocities, irrational and wanton crimes perpetrated by seemingly rational and well educated men. These crimes and terrors—superb examples of the horrors that historical processes (or the people who carry out these processes) inflict on humanity—are often accomplished in the name of god, racial and/or ideological purity, or sometimes using excuses as crass as controlling access to oil. Think, for example, of the torture instruction manuals that, by conveying the unacceptable in a legal language of administrative decisions, sought to rationalize the inexcusable.

I fear I am entering here a very difficult and dangerous territory: providing not so much examples of escaping history as of the root causes that force some people to turn their backs on the world or on history. I should not conflate the social, economic, and political maladies that have beset mankind throughout history which, after all, do not always lead to religious flight from the world, with the actual process of denying history. We should therefore return to the issue of the witch craze as an example of how early modern people embraced a set of beliefs that are, to most of us in the twenty-first century, close to delusional. But the witch craze was a clear attempt to deal with early modern uncertainties and to explicate and erase the challenges of the age.

Almost three years ago, as I was getting ready to write, after reading the morning newspapers (reading newspapers or watching the news is a sober reminder of how little we have really progressed), there was an item that called my attention and that was closely related to the matters discussed so far. It seems that there is a fundamentalist Christian church in Tennessee (still active as I write this in late 2010) that preached that soldiers killed in Iraq were the victims of god's wrath because, according to this church, the US is a country that harbors homosexuals. Improvised explosive devices, by this logic, are god's swords in meting out divine justice to a sinning nation. Following on these beliefs, some members of this particular church attended (and still attend) the funerals of soldiers killed in action in Iraq. There they shout obscenities and other niceties against dead soldiers, their families, and the country. The story made the news only because a group of bikers had been trailing the fundamentalist group and acting as a shield between the demonstrators and grieving families. (CNN website posting, February 21, 2007). As bizarre as this may sound, these actions echo millenarian movements' extreme stand in early modern Europe and their assertion that god does and will continue to intervene in history. The added frisson of homosexuality, a theme so adroitly and insidiously deployed by Republicans in recent political campaigns, brings memories of Biblical Sodom and Gomorrah, and of the religious minority's insane early views of AIDS as god's punishment on immoral and "unnatural" acts. Here, as in some of my earlier examples, religions, or to be precise, some forms of religious interpretations, provide a convenient option to the few (or the many) who see the world and historical developments as unacceptable and who posit, and work mightily for, a distinct form of life, one firmly grounded in events as the work of god or gods and of god's direct intervention in historical processes.

The Rebellion at Canudos

I could of course go on piling up examples ad infinitum. But before concluding this chapter, it may be useful to take a close look at one of those millennial outbursts, one that is curious and appealing for a variety of reasons. Under the charismatic preaching and example of an enigmatic figure named Antonio Conselheiro (the Counselor), the uprising and the long, and eventually fatal, struggle of late-nineteenth-century downtrodden peasants in the arid northeastern corner of the state of Bahía (the sertaõ), Brazil, presents us with a plethora of questions and uneasy answers. They help illuminate how movements, firmly rooted in historical circumstances, become attempts to escape history. To begin, the peasant communal rising in northeastern Brazil had direct ties, unbeknownst to most of the participants, to Sebastianism. As has been noted before, this was a widespread millenarian movement centered on the figure of King Sebastián, lost on a North African battlefield in the sixteenth century. Given a literary and prophetic life in the years after his death, Sebastianism fed on popular apocalyptic agitation, social strife, and opposition to a Spanish king on the throne of Portugal after 1580. Sebastianism did not wane after the end of Spanish rule in 1640, and its ideas of redemption and the end of history had a long shelf life on the Iberian Peninsula, in the Mediterranean, and in Brazil for the next three centuries.

One must emphasize the links that join millennial movements across time and space. It is not only that apocalyptic yearnings share common characteristics, drawing as they do from Biblical sources such as the end of time and history, god's direct intervention into history, and, depending on the movement, the ushering in of a communal society, the abolition of property, and equality. Some of these ideas are present in all apocalyptic outbursts, but there is also a kind of historical intertextuality. Elements of one movement inspired and propelled the millenarian dreams of other generations across the centuries. So did Sebastianism to a visionary old man in a remote and forgotten corner of Brazil in the late nineteenth century.

We know a great deal about the rebellion of the Canudos (the name of the group, taken from the name of the town that served as the epicenter for this revolt) that took place in the very late nineteenth century because Euclides da Cunha wrote an extraordinarily moving and precise description of the group and of its tragic denouement. Born in 1866, da Cunha witnessed early in life the final abolition of slavery in Brazil in 1888 and, one year later, when the Brazilian emperor was overthrown, the establishment of an intensely secular republican government. The latter, inspired by the positivism of August Compte, was most unsympathetic to the Church and pushed swiftly for the secularization of the country. But perhaps it is time now to tell our brief and intriguing story. The setting for this "modern" millenarian tragedy was the poor and drought-stricken interior of the state of Bahía in Brazil's still poor northeast. The *sertaõ*, as the region is known, had more than its share of bandits, impoverished peasants, and oppressive landlords. Religious agitation and apocalyptic dreams, firmly rooted in dire social and economic conditions, found a compelling voice in Antonio Conselheiro, one of those charismatic preachers and builders of churches so very common in late antiquity and the Middle Ages. A religious man operating outside the parameters of church discipline, he was prompt to use the moment to spark a fire that eventually consumed large numbers of peasants and republican soldiers in the region. When officials in the small town of Joazeiro failed to deliver lumber that Antonio had already purchased to build a church in 1896, the rebellion erupted throughout the region.

For more than two decades before 1896, Antonio Conselheiro had traveled back and forth through the backlands of Bahía, helping the poor, building churches, and collecting a wide following among the destitute who saw him as a holy man. Commanding blind loyalty from his people, he had gained effective control of the region, wresting authority from church and republican representatives, arming his followers, and getting ready to defend his community from outside forces. The sides were drawn and conflict was inevitable. The republican government sent an expedition against the rebels, only to see its troops badly defeated by Antonio Conselheiro's forces in late November 1896. Retreating to Canudos, a little town in the *sertaõ*, Antonio and his followers established what they saw as a community of saints, standing at the end of time against the godless. Resulting from the conflation of social pressures, religious exaltation, and governmental ineptitude, the rebellion of the Canudos is a perfect example of how historical events and historical transformations can trigger such responses. The deeds of the Canudos, Antonio Conselheiro's faithful followers, would be incomprehensible and bizarre were it not that such movements and reactions are common in human history. Wishing to escape from the harsh world in which they lived, driven by a misguided love for the distant and paternal emperor, and wary of republican new-fangled and secularizing liberties, the peasants and bandits of the *sertaõ* fled history in the expectation of a world beyond time, and they paid the ultimate sacrifice in doing so.

Throughout most of 1897 the republican soldiers mounted ferocious attacks on Canudos and its determined defenders. Heavy casualties on both sides mounted as Antonio Conselheiro's armies repelled every attack, forcing the Brazilian army to retreat. This was soon followed by the arrival of numerous reinforcements and the renewal of the siege. The bombardment of Canudos began in earnest in August, with artillery fire aimed mostly at the churches—symbols of the Conselheiro's activities. By September 6 of that year, the towers of the new church were battered down by cannon fire. And still the rebels held. Not even Antonio Conselheiro's death on September 22 weakened the fierce resistance. Attacks and counterattacks continued through the next two weeks until the end finally came. Some women, old people, and children, more than three hundred of them, surrendered after almost a yearlong siege and execrable conditions. The men resisted until the bitter end and not a single one was left alive. As Euclides da Cunha tells us, the "town did not surrender ... it held out to the last man."

On October 5, Canudos, having been occupied inch by inch by the invading army, had only four men left, "an old man, two other adult men, and a child, facing a furiously enraged army of five thousand soldiers." These four survivors soon fell to the army's rifle fire. Women with their babies in their hands jumped into the fires raging throughout the town. All of the 5,200 or so remaining dwellings were destroyed by the occupying army after the end of the resistance. Antonio Conselheiro's body was exhumed, beheaded, and his grim-faced head carried back to the shores of the Atlantic, "where it was greeted by delirious multitudes with Carnival joy." Today the site of Canudos lies deep underwater, as a dam has created a reservoir right over the spot where apocalyptic expectations, fierce resistance, and untold violence once took place.

The reader may wish to point out that the story of the rebellion at Canudos has been replayed many times in the past. Communities moved by millenarian expectations, resisting the forces of organized states or hegemonic religion are dime-a-dozen in history. Very much in the same vein as the story of Antonio Conselheiro and his followers at the end of the nineteenth century in a remote corner of Brazil, are the stories of the last Albigensian communities at Mont Segur in 1244, stormed by orthodox Christian armies and slain without pity, the Jews at Masada, and the Celtiberians at Numancia. Much the same occurred with the inhabitants of early modern Münster. In many respects but in a very different key did the four dozen or so followers of the Heaven's Gate cult, the helpless inhabitants of Jonestown, and David Koresh's followers at Waco, already mentioned in this chapter.

What triggers such acts of resistance? What prompts such defiance in the face of certain death? Though not always motivated by religion—patriotism often plays a role—it is clear that certain forms of religious beliefs serve as a catalyst. These apocalyptic movements, a true escape and rejection of history, are almost always heterodox in nature and stand in sharp contrast to normative historical processes. While fairly large mass movements, such as that of the Canudos or the faithful establishing of a godly kingdom at Münster have close links to shifting social and economic conditions—and their programs, whether spelled out or not, have utopian dreams (the equality of all men, the abolition of property, and, in some cases, even the abolition of the family), other small scale movements, such as Heaven's Gate, though firmly planted in specific social contexts, tend towards the bizarre and esoteric. In the end, both types offer an escape from history and its manifold terrors.

Conclusion. An Excursus

Perhaps, since this is after all very much a personal reflection on the "terror of history," or on what the telling of history means in our attempts to make sense, I should retell a story with which I always begin my class on these topics. It is a true story, though, as all stories, embellished with the passing of time. It is one that I recall vividly and that has had a powerful impact on everything that has happened to me since then. In many respects, it reflects elements of the kind of mystical experiences that were quite familiar to Francis and other mystics in late medieval and early modern Europe. Many of us have experienced such things at one time or another. The reality is that I have never been misled by apocalyptic dreams.

Although there is a certain selfish attraction to the idea that when my time to leave this world comes I would not do so alone but take all of humanity with me, I love a few people too well to wish their lives to end when mine does. I am not a mystic, but I have experienced things that reaffirm the importance of religion in providing a moment in which history and time are suspended. This is the story.

In 1971, I was a history graduate student at Princeton University. I traveled to Spain to do my research on the society and politics of medieval Burgos. From late that year until spring 1972, I dutifully did my research in old and dusty archives. I grew restless. The pervasive despair of the Castilian plain, especially in what was then Franco's Spain, darkened my mood. Burgos at that time was still a provincial city. I felt alone, unable to have a decent conversation with anyone around me. Such loneliness in the midst of people I had only found before in New York. I like the idea of being a flaneur, but Burgos was just too cold for strolling its street and gazing at its people. I hurried through my work, hoping to escape the melancholy of the Castilian heartland. Finally, at the end of April I took a train to Galicia in the northwestern corner of Spain. My research finished, I looked forward to a time of rest, to being with friends.

I had never been to Galicia before, and all my assumptions about the place were to be disproved. Some people in Castile had praised Galicia's natural beauty, while denigrating its inhabitants. It did not matter. I had friends there, and I would see the ocean, something that, having been born on an island, represents almost a physical necessity for me. After several months of implacable winter, Galicia's temperate weather was a welcome respite from the wintry harshness of Castile. I arrived in Santiago de Compostela and was immediately swept away by its mossy stones, its narrow and romantic streets, the softness and warmth of the Galicians. My friend opened his home to me. I was content. When he and his roommates went to their classes at the School of Medicine, I roamed aimlessly through the streets of the medieval core of the city. Other days I slept as late as I could. No alarm clocks, nothing to do, no responsibilities. We should all have that as adults at least once in our lifetimes.

My friends had promised me a car journey along the Galician coastline, and I was anxious to see the sea. We traveled by bus to Vigo, to the house of a German friend. He was an aesthete, a good man. He was to be our host for the weekend. After a very pleasant and relaxed Saturday, we left Vigo at first light and drove along the shore of the beautiful *rías baixas,* deep-sea inlets or fjords surrounded by bright green mountains. I gazed on mile upon mile of breathtaking beaches, unspoilt yet in the early 1970s by greedy tourists or middle-class comfort. We drove by small fishing villages with their peculiar and proud *orreos* (raised grain storage bins). I drank of the green and blue of Galicia and felt like a child who had discovered a long lost home.

Our trip was often interrupted by stops in decrepit monasteries, which our German friend described with Teutonic thoroughness. At the seaside Parador de Bayona, already quite a fancy place, we ate a monumental lunch in the extended and wonderful Spanish fashion. The rich food, the light Ribeiro wine, and the sounds of the waves intoxicated me. The day had been a delightful outing, a warm experience. I was ready to return to Vigo when our German friend insisted in driving to Mount Santa Tecla, near the border with Portugal, to see some Celtic ruins.

The mountain, covered in green woods, had been a Celtic sacred place and stood facing the Atlantic Ocean. The weather had changed rapidly, as is common in Galicia, with the sun hiding behind dark clouds pushed swiftly by strong winds. A few drops of rain began to fall. My friends, having been there before, chose to stay in the car, but they prompted me to go up the last few meters to the summit and see the view. I did not really cherish the idea of going out into the increasingly wet weather but out of politeness did so. I climbed to the peak of Mount Santa Tecla and looked out over the Atlantic, extending endlessly in front of me. To my left the River Miño meandered through green valleys, serving as the border with Portugal. Unexpectedly, I felt a sense of peace and understanding. It was as if I could see into the heart of things and understand the meaning and ways of the universe. I was at peace. Peace was within me. I had never felt such tranquility or wholeness in my being. I felt this great desire to float down the mountain into the sea. No, it was not a desire to end it all, but rather that I felt and knew that every rock, every tree leaf, every cloud, the sea itself was part of me, and that I, in turn, belonged to all of them. How can I explain that for which there are no words? Even now, almost forty years afterwards, I feel this great pressure in my heart, a sense of knowing where home is, or was, for a fleeting moment, of being one and whole with my own self. How long I stood there, I do not know. The cold rain, now turning heavy, brought me back. I descended from the top of the mountain and returned to the car where my friends were a bit anxious about my delay. I had little to say, except mumbled answers to their queries. I was extremely quiet all the way to Vigo and eventually to Santiago.

What else can I say? A year and a half later, in December 1973, I traveled from New York to Galicia on one of those impromptu trips that I could ill afford then. I flew there for just four days, most of them consumed in getting from New York to Madrid, from there to Santiago, and back. I wanted to visit the mountain once again. Accompanied by many friends, I reached the Tecla. I begged my friends to let me go up to the summit alone. The beautiful view was still there, but I sat on a stone and cried. The feeling could not be recaptured. The past remained inaccessible or only so in memory. Twice again, however, I have felt something similar in nature. Once, in the mid-seventies, while walking on one of those rare perfect spring days in Princeton, having just finished rereading *The Brothers Karamazov*, I looked at the flowers and felt, but only for the briefest of time, as if I were one with nature. The other time was on one of those early fall days in California, when the Santa Ana winds have cleaned the atmosphere and the quality of light is such that everything becomes sharp and well defined. I looked around me, and I thought I was seeing the very heart of things.

Mystics define my experiences as illuminations, not real mystical union with god, only a taste of new levels of reality. In spite of these fleeting moments of comprehending the world, I remain highly skeptical of belief, but these vivid memories are there as part of my past, unexplained and unexplainable, a reminder of the power of what Freud called "the oceanic feeling" and of the enduring human hope to understand and make meaning. Just as the single mystic travels to a place in which time, history, and the world are obliterated by the sharp and luminous reality of becoming one with god, the poor, the oppressed also ride the coattails of charismatic figures, as in the Canudos case, in a blind, often futile, and almost always fatal attempt to escape through religion their individual and collective histories. But then, of course, there are other ways to escape history. Not everyone, after all, has religion.

❊ III ❊

THE WORLD OF MATTER AND THE SENSES

"Do Not Postpone Joy"
—Bumper sticker in a wonderful little store on Columbus
Avenue, New York, that sold wind-up toys. The store closed
its doors long ago. I hope because the owner went onwards
to have joy.

IT MAY BE USEFUL TO INVOKE Boccaccio once again, as will
be done also in the next chapter. Boccaccio pinpointed with
extraordinary accuracy the manner in which his fellow citizens in Florence responded to the plague in 1348. In the preface to his *Decameron,* as has been told in the preface to this
book, he described the coming of the plague to Florence, re-
lating in vivid detail the different ways in which the plague
worked its way through Florentine society. As noted earlier,
while some prayed, marched in pious processions, embraced
the bizarre devotions generated by the Black Death's carnage,
others chose different paths. Many in Florence greedily embraced the material world and sensual pleasures. For those
whose religious beliefs had been shaken by the catastrophe
or who had little faith in the efficacy of prayers, pleasure, revelry, and excess offered an escape from the incomprehensible
terror of the plague. Their revelry, as ours does today in the

face of disasters, offered some alternative to the futility of the city's policies or to the dead end of devotional practices. In 1348 Florence, nothing worked. Many probably thought, "At least let's have fun and forget the misery on the few days we have left."

Boccaccio's own words may convey what I wish to say far better. For him, there were two types of people who embraced the material world, each in a distinct way. The first type delighted in material comfort, but always in moderation.

There were some people who thought that living moderately and avoiding

all superfluity might help a great deal in resisting this disease, and so they gathered in small groups and lived entirely apart from everyone else. They shut themselves up in those houses where there were no sick people and where one could live well by eating the most delicate of foods and drinking the finest of wines (doing so always in moderation), allowing no one to speak about or listen to anything said about the sick and the dead outside; these people lived, spending their time with music and other pleasures that they could arrange.[1]

For those who chose this course, the aim was not pleasure itself but a way of erasing the pain of the death and illness prowling the streets of Florence. Here the enjoyment of fine foods and wine, music, and delectable conversation functioned as containment, a palliative to the sickness. It was a way to survive. Others thought differently, as Boccaccio tells it.

Others thought the opposite: they believed that drinking too much, enjoying life, going about singing and celebrating, satisfying in every way the appetites as best one could, laughing,

[1] Giovanni Boccaccio, *The Decameron*, trans and ed. by Mark Mussa and Peter E. Bondella (New York: W.W. Norton, 1977) 5.

and making light of everything that happened was the best medicine for such a disease; so they practiced to the fullest what they believed by going from one tavern to another all day and night, drinking to excess; and often they would make merry in private homes, doing everything that pleased or amused them the most.[2]

Although there is still here a slight expectation of escaping the illness, the drinking and merrymaking was clearly a way out of the unbearable stress that the plague had placed on Florence's citizens.

Boccaccio's description is not exceptional. Throughout history, either as individuals or as part of a group, humans have embraced the material world, seeking solace from disasters or personal loss. Sometimes these reactions are part of complex responses that include religion as well as other elements—the material and the aesthetic—all mixed together into an unusually potent brew. Part of the attraction of most religious observances is the heady combination of several of these elements. For example, the liturgy of the Mass, and prayer itself, combine the expectation of spiritual uplift with a whole range of sensory stimuli: the act of kneeling, the smell of incense, the sounds of music, the ritualized gestures of the celebrant and congregation, the aesthetic appeals— though not always—of the sculptures, paintings, stained glass windows and of the sacred space itself. Processions, pilgrimages, the perambulation of flagellants, the immersion of saddhus and the faithful in the sacred waters of the Ganges in Varanasi and other places, the ritual circling of the Ka'aba during the annual pilgrimage or Hajj to Mecca, the rhythmic swaying of the Jewish and Muslim faithful at prayer at the Temple Wall of Jerusalem or at mosques throughout the

[2] Ibid. 5.

Islamic world are constant reminders of the physical and material aspects of religious observance. Thus, one ought to be careful about making dichotomies between the spiritual and the material, for the appeal of religion as a form of escape or as a palliative to the terrors of history is indeed deeply imbedded in the material spells of religious observance. As Evelyn Underhill showed in her old but still remarkable book on mysticism, physical beauty often triggers that awareness of oneness with God that is at the very heart of the mystical experience.[3] Such was part of the enchantment of my own experiences as related in the previous chapter; the magic of physical beauty transformed into a spiritual experience.

Embracing the Senses

What then do I mean by the embracing of the material world as a way to fend off the burdens of history? And how is that embracing any different from that other embracing that leads to belief and to religion? Clearly, I mean something else here. But in approaching this topic, I must tread carefully. Meanings are always elusive, and the closer we look at these matters the closer we get to a very different kind of reading. As I was growing up and testing different kinds of ideology, it was a commonplace to argue, for example, that communists were—specifically the old guard—fully wedded to their beliefs and to Stalinist practices, that they were, in fact, "deeply religious." That is, that ideological attachments, not unlike patriotic feelings, when deeply felt and "faithfully" observed,

---

[3] Evelyn Underhill, *Mysticism: A Study in the Nature and Development of Man's Spiritual Consciousness* (New York: New American Library, 1974). Underhill was herself a mystic, and her books present a delightful mix of true belief with impeccable scholarship.

shared many of the emotional responses one finds in religious observance or mystical raptures.

One should, although always aware that categories such as physical pleasure and religious sensibilities co-exist across porous boundaries, emphasize forms of escape from history that, while focusing on the body, aim for bodily pleasure as an answer to the uncertainties of the time. After all, we all like to live well and to enjoy the greatest possible happiness. Freud taught us long ago that nothing is as pleasurable as those sensations that derive from the body and from sensory perceptions: eating, drinking, sexual pleasure, even pain which can, in certain instances and for certain people, become a form of pleasure. But what I mean here is something beyond our daily and individual search for the satisfaction of the body. The point of departure remains, nonetheless, the bodily or physical experiences of the individual, of the self, or, in some cases, of a group of individuals. The end result of this journey is pleasure. Different cultures define, and respond to, pleasure and/or desire in different ways, but the nature of our neurological responses to certain stimuli, eating when one is hungry, drinking when one is thirsty, becoming intoxicated, having sexual intercourse, follow along a limited range of possibilities, a restricted number of sensations. Religions, or at least most of the religions of the Book, have always understood the grave dangers posed by the body and the powerful attraction of the material world. In their commandments, laws, and sacred injunctions, religions have sought to restrict pleasure and to bind the body of the believer to exacting codes of conduct and denial. The regulation, and sometimes even the condemnation of sexuality, desire, and excessive eating and drinking by many religious texts alert us to the keen understanding that excesses in some of these areas of human sensory experiences is essentially anti-religious.

"Nothing in excess" proclaimed the oracle at Delphi, for even the Greeks, who were particularly receptive to the pleasures of the flesh, understood the grave danger of giving in to desire. Augustine of Hippo, who in his remarkable *Confessions* accused himself bitterly of giving in to the temptations of the flesh—though to be perfectly frank if one reflects upon pleasure, then one is not doing a thorough job of enjoying oneself—understood that the body when it seeks its own satisfaction thinks not of god or of history. We are all conceived, I paraphrase Augustine here, in moments of irrationality, that is, in those moments of sexual climax in which thoughts of god or reason are not present. This thought follows more or less along the lines of Plato who, wary of the needs of the flesh, described sexual desires and pleasure as a "frenzy," the obfuscation of rational thought by sexual desire.

Thus, the list of cardinal sins, the Ten Commandments, and most of Deuteronomy, give us a perfect road map with which to begin our inquiry. Laid out clearly in these texts is an inventory of the forms of pleasure that distract us, place us, as individuals and as collective entities, apart from god, the social order, and history. But it is not just sets of beliefs that are threatened by the excesses of the body. Society itself is also placed in danger by the unrestricted giving in to sensory dissipation. What I am talking about here is not the normal pursuit of sensations undertaken by the average human being. The issue that concerns us is the turning of pleasure and the embracing of the material world into the sole aim of life and a means to escape the burdens of history and the tyranny of time. Except for religious fanatics, the compulsive or the obsessive, we all work hard, pray or not to god or the gods, attempt to lead more of less ethical lives, and, at times (not enough of them) indulge in a good meal, entertainment, and the pleasures of the body. Our social norms and behav-

ioral conditioning—even for those who are not religious—
provide some space for fun in early life when we are children
and adolescents, some more restricted possibilities for pleasure in our middle years when careers and family deter such
pursuits for most people, and then in our late years when we
may have the wealth or the time for the pursuit of pleasure,
many of us have neither the vigor nor the health for doing
so. Or to put it in a more blunt fashion: At the beginning we
do not really know what we are doing, for pleasure is also a
learned experience. In the middle we tend to be too busy or
caught up in the routines of our lives, building a career, having a family. At the end of our lives, our unlimited enjoyment
of the world is often hampered by bad digestion, aching knees,
incontinence, and all the disasters of old age.

But of course what I mean here by the embracing of the
material world as a form of escape from disasters and from
history's terror comes in two very specific forms. The first is
the impromptu almost visceral revelry triggered by catastrophe. Boccaccio's descriptions are insightful in that they capture a well-known reality. When confronted by the onslaught
of the plague and the mounting carnage, a substantial number of people would drink, fornicate, and engage in what
in normal times might be considered transgressive behavior.
The second of these ways of embracing of the material world
occurs at the level of the individual and his awareness of
personal loss. Great tragedies, such as the loss of a loved one,
often trigger a desire to forget by lovemaking, by the physical reminder that though the loved one may be dead, we are
still alive. Such actions, as noted earlier, challenge well-laid-
out religious injunctions. They also threaten the very fabric
of society. We have all been there more or less. In the face
of painful losses, the death of cherished friends, relatives, or
other reverses, we often turn to the flesh. We shed the careful

garments of civility and propriety, the well-learned lessons of restraints and do things that we may come to regret eventually, but which in the moment we do them take us—and our minds' troubles—away from the prevailing misery and the burdens of everyday life.

History and the World of Matter

If what I describe here is easily understood, part of our experience, part of our need for physical and emotional comfort, how can it then be postulated as an escape from history? I will argue that history and historical process are driven by a multitude of forces: social, economic, cultural, geographical, demographic, and others factors. But history is also driven by the willingness of individuals and groups to put up with a lot of grief, to sublimate their needs and desires, and to go on doing their jobs doggedly in the face of overwhelming odds. I am, of course, not saying anything new. Joseph R. Strayer said as much in a short article (his American Historical Association presidential address in the early 1970s) about the promise of the fourteenth century. How was it, he asked, that when Western medieval society was beset by the ghosts of famine, plague, war, and revolution, the basic structures of government, learning, and belief survived? They did so because countless people, as noted in the preface, kept doing their jobs. When we do not, when we escape, then we are challenging the workings of history.

I admit that at no time in the short story of mankind have we been completely tempted to revert to a world without order, a world of unlimited violence and pleasure. Sporadic episodes of such bouts of unrestrained behavior however remind us that the dream of such escapes remains a powerful force in human culture, though more often than not more of a dream than a reality. Later, I will explore some of the lesser manifestations of this mythic desire for escape from historical processes or from the ever-evolving nature of power. For now, it may just be sufficient to remember that flights into the materiality of the world come in two forms: in small doses almost every one of us indulges in some form of physical pleasure. Such indulgence functions as the body's natural and necessary response to the stress of everyday life. And then there are those unique moments in which the fabric of the quotidian, the assurances provided by social structures, fall down. Left to our own devices, we flee responsibility and the future while gulping down the here and now. This second response is most often a collective one. It was what many of Florence's citizens, and people in other places in Western Europe did when battered by the plague in 1348.

Catastrophic events or the unbearable tedium and anxieties of everyday life however are not the sole motivation for such denial of everything but the present moment. Awareness of the futility of our lives, again both individual and collective, may lead us in many different ways—to religion, to aestheticism, to the senses. In the ancient world religion was often deeply bound with the body and the pleasures and sensations of the body. One could engage in Bacchic debauchery and still be observing a religious duty and ritual. It was not until the rise of asceticism, already implicit in Plato but forcefully articulated from the second century of the Christian era onwards, that the view that the body and the material world are corruptible and evil took a foothold in the West. Thus, we should not be deceived by historians who plot the development of Western history along the line of great intellectual achievements. Bacchic celebrations, the highly ritualized and intoxicating release of all the passions in violent outbursts of promiscuous and festive behavior, formed an integral part of the classical world. For every Socrates, Plato, or Aristotle, there were hundreds who joined in these communal activities, undertaken with the tacit approval of the authorities. What did happen on these occasions?

Bacchic celebrations were not exceptional events or simply bizarre aspects of Classical culture. Temple prostitute cults in the ancient Fertile Crescent are examples of other alternate forms of belief based upon the body. The ancient and semi-mythic polity of Sybaris, a place where, according to reports, citizens gave themselves over completely to pleasure and luxury as the central organizing principle of their lives, is yet another a reminder of the powerful attraction of pleasure as a counterweight to social and political rules, religious principles (or as part of them), and the growing stifling control of states. As noted earlier, most laws and religions (certainly the religions of the Book) aim to forbid and to punish these types of behavior: from eating too much to sexual behavior. But historical evidence always tells us that the attraction of excessive behavior is powerful indeed. Literary representations of dissolution reflect these common and well-known types of lives.

In the Realm of the Senses and Artistic Representations of the Pleasures of the Body

It may seem a bit confusing to range from Bacchic revelry to a fairly well-known Franco-Japanese cult film (*In the Realm of the Senses*, 1976) that very graphically depicts what I am trying so hard and, probably so unsuccessfully, to convey here. The film made quite an impact when first shown by reason of its frank depiction of a real 1930s event. A man and woman withdraw from the world and engage in continuous, violent, sadistic, and suicidal sexual intercourse, ending with the strangulation of the male, his penis being cut, and his body inscribed in blood. While every sexual position is explored (and exploited), what always impressed me about the film was not its erotic elements—after all, after a while, the sheer pain and rising violence of continuous coupling become almost unbearable. (Was it envy that made it unbearable?) What struck me forcefully instead were both the setting (isolation from the world outside) and the attempts by the real couple and by the actors impersonating them to erase time and history. In that room, the only thing that mattered was not just making love, but extracting every ounce of pleasure, pain, and possession. The world outside vanished, time vanished, history vanished. And since this could not be sustained, then death was the only logical conclusion rather than a return to the "normal" world. While most of us will not take sexual encounters to this fatal conclusion, it is clear that most of us have been, even if fleetingly, there at one time or another. That is, at a point in which the physicality of the act seems to throw a veil over other parts of our lives. In the moment, the moments, in which there is no thought, no reason, no god, no history. Of course, we cannot keep it up. We consciously move away from the brink. We return to the routines of everyday life. We put our masks on once again. But we would be lying if we did not admit that we have seen the countryside beneath the cliff where we stood, been mesmerized by the power of the flesh, made to forget, made reluctant ever to leave the room even if remaining there would bring an unavoidable death. The movie, like all movies, is a fictional representation. The story, nonetheless, is real—and enticing. This did happen. Things like this do happen, again and again.

Something of this feeling, even if rendered in less graphic sexual form, can be found in Gottfried von Strassburg's *Tristan.* In this very early courtly romance, Tristan and Isolde escape into the woods, into a crystal cave, both a temple of love and a place outside the world and time. There they literally, in the metaphorical language of the poet, feed on each other, feed on love. What makes this description so moving is that Gottfried lets us know, in an earnest authorial aside, that such caves did exist. That he had been there. That he wrote about what Tristan and Isolde experienced sexually and romantically from first hand acquaintance. That he also knew of that all-consuming physical and emotional love that denies the world outside and the flow of history and time itself.

Milder forms of attempting to capture the nature of pleasure, not always successfully, can be found even in the ancient world. As Republican Rome became a distant memory, and the new power of emperors imposed tyrannical and arbitrary rules, intellectuals sought escape in fictional (though based upon lived or perceived events) accounts as a way to endure the irrational demands of rulers such as Caligula or Nero (both emperors of the first century of the Common Era). Petronius Arbiter's striking *Satyricon*, above all his *Feast of Trimalchio* (a chapter of the *Satyricon*) is a very good example of this new satirical genre that, while engaging in social criticism of the nouveaux riches and of their foreign extraction, also presented a vivid picture of how to escape the suffocating demands of new imperial power.

Petronius, we are told in Tacitus' somber account of the decline of imperial dignity, was asked to commit suicide by the emperor, not an uncommon request in that New Rome, and we are also told that he "opened his veins in a warm bath, while music and beautiful slaves eased his way into that great beyond from which no one has ever really returned." But what was the feast of Trimalchio all about? What were those sensual moments that animated it? In many respects, Trimalchio's feast, as do feasts today, brought Bacchic excesses out of the woods and open landscapes into urban interior spaces. Most of our feasts today, even weddings (which are often marked by excessive eating, vigorous dancing, epithalamics, and symbols of fertility) are pretty sedate affairs in which the burdens of civility and propriety prevent us from behaving true to form. The few who, in their intoxication, make spectacles of themselves, are promptly removed for their lack of propriety. But all our celebrations have within them a bit of the Bacchic and a lot of transgressive behavior waits, ready to emerge.

Trimalchio's Feast

In reality, Trimalchio's feast was a pretty dull affair, as most feasts are in the end, with little of the Bacchic and much of the ostentation and vulgarity of new money, or, to be fair, with Petronius' perception of a despised new social class. A succession of bizarre and supposedly expensive foods and wines, a whiff of homoeroticism, boring storytelling of some exceptionally piquant tales, etc. When threatened with yet a further extension of the feast, the narrator flees to safety. In many respects, the feast reminds us of our shared experiences of revelry, of the Dionysian moment when the boundaries of the self are breached and we become one with the world and with those celebrating around us. But in the final analysis, we are more often than not disappointed, as the festivities become dreadful and boring affairs in the mold of Trimalchio's feast. But let's think of the Bacchic as still alive in our own world. Think of the sixties or of youthful raves today, those mysterious events on the edges of normal middle-class propriety, about which we, the old, hear only at second hand.

95

They are the events in which our children and grandchildren may be participants and from which we, because of our age, are rightfully banned. I am told by my students of the loud music, the endless dancing and singing, the occasional use of psychotropics—mostly Ecstasy. No longer wild frenzies in the woods of Thrace or outside Rome, modern raves are held in huge decrepit halls, or, as is the case in California, in the desert. History and the burdens of the present dissolve to the beat of frenzied music. Woodstock, once again, the fortieth anniversary of which we celebrated recently, was a gigantic rave *avant la lettre*. All of those who lived through the sixties, either as participants or interested observers recognize the appeal of these communal celebrations, even though today's raves are, in many respects, quite different from the sixties' ideologically charged movements. While in the sixties such communal gatherings had a strong political edge, raves today are apolitical; in fact, they may be one of the strongest statements about the move away from the political and the desire to escape from engaging history.

Very much like Bacchic celebrants, those attending raves, after an entire night of celebrations (it must be an exhausting affair), go back to their classrooms, to their part-time jobs, marking time until the next big event. So it is not just sex, food, or drink that releases us from time and history. Anyone who likes music or who likes to dance can sympathize with the forces at work in these types of celebrations. They have to be sympathetic toward what happens to both body and mind when caught up in the beat of music. I am not talking here of course of the aesthetic pleasure—most of it based upon a learned appreciation of music, but on the relation of music to the movement of the body. Somewhat paraphrasing Nietzsche's descriptions of the Dionysian rituals in his *The Birth of Tragedy*, I think here of vigorous dancing in which the body moves not in a predetermined way but sways and gyrates to the beat of the music. And then the dancer becomes one with all the other dancers, swept away in the rhythm of the music, the physical exertion, a kind of intoxicating feeling—I am sure that there is some very convincing chemical explanation—that liberates us from our inhibitions and taboos, that, while joining us to others, paradoxically isolates us, even if only momentarily, from the world around us.

Carnival

Carnival, or at least some forms of Carnival, have often provided a setting in which to lose the self in collective revelry. In doing so, one, and the community of celebrants as well, transcend time and place. Carnivals are of course historical phenomena, and today most are pretty domesticated and scripted affairs. Rio's famous Carnival is an outstanding example of bourgeois propriety. It is planned years in advance. Each *escola* (school) of Samba works dutifully, preparing its "fantasies," that is, its distinctive costumes. They march within a rigidly set time frame. Their performances are judged according to a whole series of set criteria: such as costumes, the time that it takes to perform the dances, quality of the music, originality, etc. The only thing lacking is spontaneity. I remember seeing, as an adolescent, the Carnival in La Habana, which, not unlike the Carnival in Salvador (Bahía, Brazil) today, was neatly divided into two related but antithetical parts. On Sunday afternoon lavishly decorated floats paraded in a carefully delimited space, while middle-class families gazed from stands reserved and paid for in advance. It was colorful. It was fun somewhat. It was certainly not wild or subversive. On Saturday evening late at night, the Carnival schools came out and marched through the streets. Scantily clad women and men danced, while enervating Afro-Cuban music filled the air. Standing on the sidewalk and drinking heavily, the crowd waited to be swept along by their favorite group or music, joining extemporaneously in the dancing and singing, ending up often in a promiscuous letting go of all inhibitions.

Of course, these two different modes of celebrating were also grounded in age, class, and, in Cuba and Brazil, race. The crowd on Sunday afternoons was mostly white, well to do, and middle-aged. They dreamed of the Carnival that stood for breaking away from their well-regulated lives, but they seldom had the will to let go fully. Those who came on Saturday evening were mostly black, poor, and young, with a few young middle-class men slumming among those with whom they had little or no contact during the rest of the year. I, who because of age and inclination, moved between the two worlds, attended the Saturday evening celebrations because they were so much more fun, but I also joined my family on Sunday outings as befitted my social status. In some ways, and serendipitously, this excursus into the politics of Carnival leads us back into a reflection on class and an even more poignant discussion of its association with the embracing of material objects and pleasure. It also foreshadows some of the discussion to follow in chapter 4 on the aestheticizing of historical catastrophes.

Pleasure and Culture

If, as Socrates argued, the unexamined life is not worth living, then Bacchic frenzies, raves, Carnival revelry, and other such popular and heightened forms of embracing physical pleasure are a forceful denial of that philosophical maxim and of long held ideals about the rational life and culture. And they echo Nietzsche's elegant dichotomy between the Dionysian (a form of Carnivalesque intoxication) and the Apollonian, that is, that we live in permanent tension between rational individualism and our yearning for community and the transcendental obliteration of the self. In short, wild celebrations formed not by small group of intellectuals but by common people seem to have far more vitality and popularity than the seeking of the reflective life. In a circuitous fashion, this leads us to the question of who is, in fact, escaping history. While we are all essentially historical actors, whether fully exercising our agency and impacting the historical process, whether we are subjects of history and history is imposed on us, or whether we write it, the reality is that for the immense majority of mankind history and historical events are often extraneous to their daily life or outside their conscious field of experiences. The differences in how we experience terrifying catastrophes are deeply imbedded in class distinctions, economic well-being, and education. For most people on earth the most important things are those that are part of their individual and familial experiences, grounded in the local and immediate, and not in the long sweep of history. In Eliade's essay on the terror of history, he described how many chose or were pushed into leading a subhuman or marginal existence as one of the ways to shut out the angst of being part of historical events. The problem with this of course, as noted earlier, is that marginality is rarely chosen. More often than not it is imposed on us, Francis of Assisi and other mystics notwithstanding. It is, with noted exceptions, the result of specific social, economic, political, and even cultural circumstance.

A powerful literary representation of such a situation and a salutary reminder of the importance of social class in this discussion can be found in George Orwell's frightening novel, *1984.* A book of deep social and political impact—an impact somewhat diffused by its compulsory reading in high school —*1984*, in which the ultimate aim of the Inner Party is to "freeze history," presents a thoughtful depiction of a society where the majority of the population, the "proles," while conscripted as soldiers, bent by propaganda, facing the scarcity and squalor of everyday life and Big Brother's brutal regime, retained nonetheless a liveliness denied to the ruling party. In a moving scene, the protagonist Winston Smith, after renting a room on top of a small, dilapidated shop in the proles' quarter—a room supposedly without a telescreen and thus away from the intrusive vigilance of the party—looks into the adjacent yard at a woman doing her washing and singing. The image of this cheerful woman, an archetypical "earth mother" figure, is a telltale sign of the enduring vitality of many of those for whom the terror of history makes no dent in the small pleasures of the quotidian, and for whom the simple and elaborate pleasures of the material world stand— in this case washing, hanging the clothes to dry, and singing some rubbishy but catchy tune—as bulwarks against the horrors of history.

Here again, as we stumble into an understanding of how men and women face historical events, one must admit that not everyone historicizes events, that historically an awareness of a distance between oneself in the past and oneself in the present is not a given. Reflection on the past, on time, and on the relation of our individual and collective selves to evolving history is perhaps a rare commodity. Most of mankind lives in the present, and the past plays out like a moving kaleidoscope of small and particular personal memories. And of those individual remembrances, those that are most powerful for the many are those associated with the body and the experiences and pleasures of the body: the great meal, the great feast, that first or an unforgettable sexual encounter, and the like.

At the intersection of memory and history, we should not deny the fact that many escape from, or refuse to, confront the heavy burdens of human history or to historicize their collective experiences. Rather, the rejection of or neglect of history is perhaps the only way in which the majority of mankind can cope with the cascade of "bad news" that assails us every day of our lives. And that is not even thinking of the real disasters, such as plagues, famines, ethnic cleansing, all-out war, terrorist attacks, and other common occurrences of this sort. Writing notes for this chapter on April 18, 2006, a date when forty-five years ago I was in a prison in Cuba and not feeling very pleased with the world, I glanced at the front page of the *New York Times*. The news was not comforting. Flanking two photographs—one of an Israeli medic tending to a victim of a terrorist attack and the other of the young suicide bomber, allegedly twenty-one years old but looking more like fifteen—the headlines described a suicide bombing in Tel Aviv, the adverse health impact of Hurricane Katrina on storm evacuees, ruined treasures in Babylon, a former governor of Illinois found guilty of graft, the police in New York City turning to horses to control crime, and last but not least, news about changes in presidential advisers at the White House, Mr. Bush being, of course, the greatest catastrophe of them all. And it is not as if yesterday's front page was any better, nor should we expect better tidings tomorrow.

As I reread and revise this chapter, the news is about the oil spill affecting the long-suffering Gulf Coast, the deepening fiscal crisis, the growing number of casualties in Afghanistan. And these are just the main items. I fear however that most people will be far more interested in Le Bron James' decision about where to play basketball for the next five years than in any solution to any of these monumental crises. And it is not as if the majority of the population was uncaring or marginal. The casual newspaper reader is confronted by such a deluge of bad and/or tasteless news every day of his or her life that it should not be surprising that turning to the sports or entertainment sections for some respite from the daily accumulation of woe is one of the ways we all cope with the heavy toll of daily events.

Living In and Outside of History

Living in an age in which many people (certainly in this country) are alienated from the past, and where the majority of the population tends (or seems) to live in an endless present, most of the people in the world escape history by turning their backs on the wreckage of humankind—Benjamin's pile of debris to which the angel of history wishes to put a stop. True, embracing the quotidian, the small pleasures of everyday life, the fortunes and misfortunes of one's favorite sport team, gambling, drinking, and sexual pleasures as dominant activities of one's life are fairly mild escapes; none of these things have the spectacular quality of a Bacchic orgiastic celebration, Carnival, or a rave. After all, it would be fairly impossible to live in a permanent Carnival. Nonetheless, the choice of whether to live within history or outside of it is one seldom taken in a conscious manner. When choosing the latter, however; that is, when choosing to live outside history, most people do so by embracing the material world.

I should hasten to add that such an assertion does not constitute a moral or ethical judgment. The world is not divided into those who accept, fight, or are active agents in the workings of history, and those who do not. One is not really superior to the other. As a younger person, I decried what I perceived to be the mindless escape into sports, drinking, commodities, and sex. But I have slowly come to the painful realization that whether consciously or unconsciously, such behavior is as good a strategy as any other. Of course, there is often not one single path. Those who eagerly embrace the physicality of the world may later in life opt for religion as a palliative or vice versa. Peter Abelard, the well-known twelfth-century theologian, philosopher, and fabled lover of Heloise, embraced a life of chastity after his castration. What else could he do? But even without such radical intervention, our nature is to change. I do not make therefore rigid distinctions between those who understand and those who do not that the history that humans shape is often cruel and that our response is often to flee or to resist history through a myriad of sensory routes. Those who turn inwards to the unfolding of their individual or communal lives, that is, those who live in the moment by seeking bodily pleasures may not be misguided after all. There is a great deal to be said for living in the moment with no reference to either past or future. I often tell my students that they should not postpone joy. Although unfortunately I do not always follow my own advice, the thought is sound and to be taken directly to heart.

I do not know whether this explanation is fully satisfactory or not. Allow me another try and to attempt to deal with the issue in simpler terms. There are some who reflect on history and its outcomes and realize that by their actions as historical agents they seek either to alter the course of history, to deflect it, to resist it, or to escape from it. Some even try to render history into writing and thus direct it into some discernable ideological or rational channels. Some do these

things or several of them at the same time, fully and ratio-
nally engaged in their individual and collective efforts to live
within historical processes; others are only partially conscious
of their actions. And there are still others who do not think
about these matters at all, but rather choose to live in the
world they have found, perhaps only attempting to improve
those circumstances that directly affect them. If you are reading this book, you will most probably think that to be in the
first group is "better," for at least we have some agency, some
ability to chose, to set different courses, but do we? The conundrum here is whether to ignore history—though history
most certainly does not ignore us, and it is often unforgiving
of our neglect—may not be after all far less demanding of
our time and strength and lead to far less grief and to more
pleasure.

Of course, one may shut one's self out of the pile of catastrophes growing skyward in front of the angel of history by
being caught up in sweeping apocalyptic or religious movements, in Bacchanalian excesses, and/or in Carnivalesque
revelry. Nonetheless, while one may be able to escape history
ephemerally through such activities, the real secret is to make
them one's sole life. That is, to arrange things so that there
will be nothing outside either the single-minded concentra-
tion on living in the moment or in a permanent (difficult to
do in any case) state of intoxication. This often leads to an
early demise, but, in the end, we all wind up in the same
place. We all end up dead. In the end, only memory, that is,
the memory of what we have done, remains. In that sense,
it may be worthwhile to revisit Socrates' statement on the
examined life. In that sense, including both the manner in
which some confront (rather than escape) history and the
manner in which we seek to be remembered, the examined
life is truly worth living for no other reason than that it is a

life that at least provides a possibility of understanding the links that bind us to history, to historical process, even if very few humans can continuously reflect on these matters without some respite, thus Carnival, religion, the great feast of Bacchus.

Love

Though it may seem far from ideas about embracing the world and a life of the senses, I wish to discuss a topic here that conflates my earlier and artificial categories of religion, the embracing of the material world, and aesthetics as ways to escape history. Throughout human experience, love has always provided a forceful antidote to the terror of history. We should think of love as sets of variegated experiences. Sexual attraction and romantic love are different but interconnected ways of placing one's self if not outside history altogether, at least in a position to temporarily cancel it. I do not speak here of course of the normal working out of our libido or the affection and love that may grow up with companionship. Most often people imagine or posit two forms of love. One consists of sexual experiences, the sort of stuff we saw earlier in the discussion of the film *In the Realm of the Senses*. The other is what we may call "romantic" love. Both forms, whether a purely sexual or an idealized romantic love, whether individual or collective, seek in their most exalted expressions to obliterate the self, to create a union, much as mysticism aims at a union with god. One form, the working out of naked sexual desire, is often suppressed or censored in society as too dangerous and subversive. The other, romantic love, has filled, and continues to fill, the pages of romance and Western literature. One form of articulating love does not exclude the other, although in Western societies there have long been powerful attempts to see these two kinds of love as antithetical.

For reasons that are quite complex and that will require a long and complicated explanation, we have long held to the idea that matter and spirit, or mind and body, or body and soul were different entities, often at war with each other. Already in Plato we get a strong sense of that struggle, and it grows stronger in Plotinus. Christianity of course absorbed with a vengeance this idea of the enduring struggle between flesh and spirit, positing the soul as a prisoner of the body. The body in turn drags us inexorably into damnation. During the heroic first centuries of Christianity the cure was, more often than not, asceticism and denial. The staying power of these ideas is quite remarkable. Voltaire, who powerfully described history as "nothing more than a tableau of crimes and misfortunes," wickedly also denounced virginity. He wrote in a letter to Marriott in 1766: "It is amusing that virtue is made of the vice of chastity; and it's a pretty odd sort of chastity at that, which leads men straight into the sin of Onan, and girls to the waning of their color." And of course a recent candidate to the senate in Delaware would have been for virginity and against even the sin of Onan. The great Augustine of Hippo, in an equally wicked aside, implored god in the *Confessions*: "Give me chastity and continency—but not yet!"

The modern and often repeated statement, "you love me only because of my body," meaning that what you seek from the other person is sensual satisfaction without any semblance of affection or romantic attachment, captures fully the sense that there are two kinds of love, the sensual and the spiritual. This is of course sheer nonsense, since one is one's body and memory and little else, and there is no such thing as a separate mind and body. Yet, we persist in our delusion and often embrace a hierarchy of love. Romantic or "spiritual" love we always place on a higher stage than the naked desire of the flesh. I know exactly what I am talking about, since, nourished by nineteenth-century romantic novels, including such desperate earlier works as Goethe's *The Sorrows of Young Werther*, I also fostered such beliefs and held on to them passionately and quite irrationally. Although today, I know that loving the body, and what we emotionally call the heart, are the complements of a single passion, nonetheless, rereading, as I am doing at present, most of the books I read between the ages of eleven and sixteen, I am struck by the enduring power of romantic fantasies, and by the manner in which they shaped who I am and how I think.

Romantic and "Spiritual" Love

It may be easier to examine these two types of love, the sensual and the romantic, even if in essence they are one, as discrete categories. After all, in forgetting history through love and passion, most humans have made that distinction. Once again I would like to bring this to the personal level and ask your indulgence to tell yet another story about myself.

Between 1978 and 1989, I wrote a short story once a year. I wrote these stories as a form of therapy and as an escape from the usual despair of my life. In many respects, they may qualify as aesthetic escapes, even though they certainly lack any literary value. These stories also provided me with an opportunity to give vent fully to my romantic yearnings, cultivated since adolescence, as noted earlier, by an unhealthy diet of books by Alexandre Dumas, Victor Hugo, Goethe, Sir Walter Scott, and others. The stories varied with the year and with whether I was ready to write them or not. One about my father's death kept being postponed until it burst out of me. Instead, that year I wrote a semi-humorous story about Cubans going to airports. Usually, I wrote these very short stories at a sitting, did not revise them, and sent them to a few friends as a Christmas card. They often combined autobiographical sketches with fictionalized details. The stories varied, but essentially they were variations on the themes of longing, desire, and redemption through love. They were stories about my sadness and sense of being totally lost. One particular story had a tremendous impact on my life. So here it is.

The Eve of Santa Barbara

On the eve of Santa Barbara 1981, I took a train from Paris to Venice. I had been invited to give a paper in France, and although I could never turn down an opportunity to visit Paris, the request had come at a most inconvenient time. My school term in New York had not ended; thus, thanks to the kindness of one of my colleagues who covered my classes, I had one week for the entire journey. Having delivered my paper and with still four free days ahead of me before my return, I decided, on a kind of desperate, last chance romantic impulse to travel to Venice. It was, to begin with, an irrational act, the sort of act one undertakes at the onset of greater responsibilities, when the world begins to close around and burden one's life. Since I could not afford a plane ticket from Paris to Venice—those were the days before Easyjet and Ryan Air—I had to travel by train, leaving the Gare de Lyons at 8 PM, arriving in Venice at 8 AM the next day, walking through the city for twelve hours and then taking a train back to Paris at 8 PM. I remember well the day because a few hours after my departure the course of my life was radically changed and because the vigil and day of Santa Barbara, December 3rd and 4th, have long been associated in memory with mysterious and romantic events.

As a young man in Cuba, on the eve of Santa Barbara many years ago, my friends and I roamed the streets of our hometown. All through the town and the island, the *santeros*, the priests of *Santería*, the syncretistic religion that emerged from the fusion of African and Christian beliefs, opened their houses to all comers. Immense amounts of food and liquor were served on that day, and the drums, their goatskins stretched tight over fire, played a constant and intoxicating ritual beat. The incense, the music, the sensual dancing were believed to bring the *orixas*, the gods, down to earth where they would enter the bodies of the dancers, though I often saw *santeros* and others in the celebrations possessed by alien and unfriendly spirits.

The whole feast revolved around the deity being honored that day. In the most prominent place in the *santeros*' house, covered with gold, silver, and rich red fabrics, with fruit offerings in front of her, stood always the statue of Santa Barbara, the patroness of artillerymen and mistress of thunder and lightening in the old Catholic list of saints. But she is also the powerful, gender-changing, dark, and mysterious Chango, goddess supreme of the Afro-Cuban pantheon. I, who attended these festivals with an armor of skepticism, detached curiosity, and even disdain—I was after all a very devout Catholic then—always had on that night a vague premonition of magical fulfillment. At the age of fourteen, on the eve of Santa Barbara and the early hours of her feast, I had a most vivid, almost real, vision. I saw the face of a woman, dark, mysterious, with sensuous and inviting lips. She was, in my mind, the essence of life itself, a primeval and vital force of nature. She came without words, took my face in her hands, and kissed me deeply and fully on the lips. She then put her hands on my chest and said, "You are mine," and in her kisses, my life, my self ebbed away. Throughout my adult life, I often recalled that dream-like vision with some alarm at the loss and vanquishing of the center of my being, yet also longing for such surrender of the heart, for being swept away by passion and love. For many years I sought and waited for her. She never came. But on the eve of Santa Barbara, it often seemed as if her presence, her spirit, were alive in me, as if her kindred soul was there waiting to be one with me.

In this manner, with a vague sense of expectation many years later on the eve of Santa Barbara, I waited in the early evening for my train to depart from the Gare de Lyons. Unable to purchase a second-class sleeping berth, I searched through the train for an empty compartment and, having found one, tried to project an air of unpleasantness as a deterrent to unwanted company. I settled down with a few books and a handbag, a bottle of wine, bread, cold cuts, and cheese, hoping for a quiet trip, a few hours of sleep, and blessed Venice. By the time the train had reached the outskirts of Paris, a young woman ambled in from the corridor and inquired politely in a barely English-accented Italian if there was room for her. Not reluctantly I answered in English that yes, the compartment was quite empty and that she was most welcome to take a seat. I helped with her luggage, placing it in the overhead rack. She took her coat off and sat across from me. We exchanged the usual pleasantries and half-hearted introductions of travelers recently met. Now I was able to examine her carefully. She was young, yet fully a woman, deeply tanned, with sensuous lips and a strong, agile body. Her legs, hips, her whole body was an image of suppleness and grace, a reminder of ideals of beauty long forgotten. Her English revealed her as an American, but she looked Mediterranean, a dream out of Sefarad, hundreds of years ago. She smiled with ease, effortlessly, and I thought of lines from Byron right away.

> A mind at peace with all below,
> A heart whose love is innocent.

Alas! She truly "walked in beauty like the night of cloudless climes and starry skies." In a few minutes, the liveliness of her speech and gestures erased years from my shoulders, brought a playful grin to my lips, and a cure to my chronic melancholy. We discovered that our destinations were quite similar. She was stopping at Mestre to see friends and then continuing to Venice. We had, of course, both been to Venice before and loved the city equally, though for very different reasons. It was not difficult to fall into easy conversation. Filled with that desire to please and agree that often marks the beginning of friendship, we were certain to pinpoint music we both liked, events and books we both had shared, places we both had visited and loved. Yet, besides our mutual desire to please one another, there was also an unusual degree of commonality. I was certain I had always known her; she seemed a long lost friend suddenly rediscovered. As the train sped into the night, the small compartment filled with a glow, a sense of comfort and peace.

She offered me bread, almost ritualistically, from the loaf she was carrying in her large handbag, and I accepted, pointing to the traditions of sharing bread and salt that binds nomads in lasting friendship—nomads such as the two of us, wandering the roadways of Europe. "We shall now be friends," I said to her, "bound together by old customs and immemorial traditions." I opened my bottle of wine, that I had been saving to drink by myself in Venice, and we communed with bread and wine, drinking from the same cup, eating from the same loaf of bread. Half jokingly, half seriously, for it was Friday, I remarked that the only thing missing was for her to light candles and for me to recite from the Song of Songs, and, thus, to complete the rituals of the Sabbath night. "Or perhaps," I added, we are reenacting the Old Christian celebration of the *agape*. I repented immediately of my flippancy and of what she may have understood as an advance. I was not interested, not that night, not with her, in a casual encounter, or in the embarrassment and awkwardness of a half-meant sexual advance. I feared to break the spell of this very special night in which dreams become reality. Yet, as I looked at her, she truly reminded me of the Song of Songs. I could almost hear her singing, "I am as dark but lovely, oh, daughters of Jerusalem, as the tents of Cedar, as the curtains of Salma."

We changed the tone of our conversation, she with a smile, gracefully avoiding any misunderstanding. Looking at the books I carried with me, she recognized some and asked about the others. I was rereading Flaubert's *Sentimental Education*, and while pointing out that she had read *Madame Bovary*, she also confessed to not being familiar with the former.

"What is that book all about? Is it as good a book as *Madame Bovary*?" she asked.

"It is a book about the end of illusion, about the death of love," I answered, in the highly stylized and almost outdated and sentimental way in which I often speak. "I have always read this book in special moments of my life, when the intoxication of early love comes to an end, when passion is replaced by unbelief and regret. The *Sentimental Education* is truly about an unsentimental education. I have spent most of my life posing as a romantic and an idealist, but I am neither. Having loved or thought myself to have been in love, having done all the foolish things that lovers do, having trembled and cried from, and for, love, in the end I have discovered only emptiness, only the regrets of paths not followed."

She interrupted me at that moment to protest and vehemently to deny my words. "Surely," she added, "there is life in being in love, and a feeling of renewal that cannot be dismissed and that cannot be forgotten, even after love is gone." Emphasizing, in an almost avuncular fashion, our different ages and experiences, I answered that it was perhaps correct for one so young to speak as she had done, but that sometime or another all love must come to an end. All the agonies and pleasures of those first weeks, first months, I explained, are soon replaced by the routines of every day, by the commonplace banalities of the quotidian, by the vulgarity of things that are not permanent. "I do realize," I continued, "that the feelings of those special moments cannot be maintained, I can even accept the quiet placidity of two people living together in harmony and love over a long period of time, even for life. But, personally, I feel deeply the deception, the sense of betrayal that is involved in every romantic relationship. I must confess to you that even in the most intense love affairs, while I sought from the other person complete attention, complete dedication, the self within me resisted fusion, resisted surrender. There was a point beyond which I could not go; I was always much too conscious of the separation between myself and the person I professed to love. Love seeks to make two people into one; yet at the peak of emotion, an element of skepticism, of doubt, has always gnawed at my heart. I find a part of me looking cynically, detachedly, at my actions, at my words. Perhaps, there is something dry and dead within me. Perhaps the problem is not love, but me.

113

Look, my friend, please look and listen to the language of lovers, a language that I have used and misused liberally. It is full of treacherous words, empty and meaningless promises. Come on! We all know that in the end all of us catch on to such deception. We come to understand the uselessness of words in the face of our actual deeds. I think that was exactly what Mozart wanted to say in *Cosi fan tutti*, except that, fools that we are, we ignore the truth and glorify the lovers in the opera.

With pain and surprise in her eyes, she argued with me. "You cannot believe what you have just said. You do not mean it at all. How can you live without love? How can you exist without dreams? You must not do so," she emphatically added.

"My dear," I responded, "I have done so for years. I have refused to give of myself. I have turned my back on all those occasions that might lead to infatuations or to love. I seek no adventures. I am cautious. The suffering of love, or what is even worse, the agony of seeing and experiencing the end of love, of building an ideal to see it fall apart within me is far too painful. I do not wish to have, to experience this any-more. I shall take no more chances. There is perhaps indiffer-ence in my life, but there is also dull stability, work, duty. I cannot bear to find myself turning against my words. There is no love forever; there is no constancy. Perhaps there is for others, but not for me. It is a curse, the bane of my life, to wish to love forever and to be incapable of doing so."

Her beautiful light-brown eyes were now almost covered with tears. She rose from her seat, took my face in her hands and, bending over me, kissed my lips with kisses from her mouth. I sat in the train compartment as if pieces of my being were being wrenched from me. She reached deep into the center of my self and swept away all resistance. Lost in her eyes, in her lips, I was defenseless, no longer conscious of myself. She took my glasses off and kissed my eyes softly.

"Io te amo," she whispered, "Io te amo."

And I answered, "Io te amo anche. Sempre."

I stood up, facing her. Looking into each other's eyes, we were unwilling to utter any sound. We were incapable of words. I understood as never before the shortcomings of speech. I did not wish to use sentences, words spoken before and never meant. Sacrilege! For no words could capture my feelings then. With my eyes closed, I ran the tip of my fingers over her bare arms, and she trembled. Confused, I did not know how to react, what to do or not to do. It was as if previous patterns of behavior, previous lives, had suddenly been discarded. It was as if something entirely new and different were now expected of me. I feared that a false gesture, an untimely word would take her away from me. On that night, this child of nature woke me up to a new life, and I knew then certitude and peace. She pointed with her finger to where her neck began and asked me to kiss her there. I did. Touching her soft skin lightly with my tongue, I felt, after an entire life of control, of self-sufficiency, my intense need for her, a longing I would always carry with me. A longing that was both a burden and a joy.

She repeated in Italian: "Io te amo." She paused and added, "but I must now leave. I cannot be with you. I cannot stay. Smile, be glad of this moment, treasure it. Please remember me as I have been today. Remember what I have said to you today. Remember that I do love you. Love me always." I nodded silently. With my eyes fixed on her, trying to imprint her whole being forever in my memory, I saw how she took her bag and left the compartment without any additional words, with a sweet and loving smile. I thought of following her. I could not. I collapsed on the seat, put my face into my hands, and began to cry.

The Aftermath

I wrote this story in the fall of 1982, one of my annual stories. The story wove true events: it blended the real story of the vision I had on the eve of Santa Barbara in Cuba at age fourteen (remember that fourteen in Cuba almost half a century ago is not the same as fourteen today in the US) with the fictional account of an encounter in the train to Venice, though the trip to Venice was also true. Written almost three decades ago, when I was in the midst of pressing personal crises, the story was a painful remembrance of long-held dreams and of a romantic and hopeless desire for love, but it was also a hope of escape, even if brief, from what had become the burdensome ennui of my life. But, in 1987, the dark woman of my dreams did come, not in dreams and fantasies, but in reality. She was as I had described her five years earlier: soft light-brown eyes, tanned, supple, lively, a daughter of Zion. I shared all my stories with her, and she liked this one best and wrote a sort of different ending to my awfully romantic denouement. Later, she asked me what day the feast of Santa Barbara was and when did I have my vision. When I told her the date and hour, we discovered that it was precisely the day, hour, and year of her birth. It was such an eerie coincidence, what people sometimes call fate. And to complicate matters even further, her name is Scarlett, meaning "red," the color of Chango, the *orixa* or African deity whose feast falls on December 4th. More than twenty years later, we still share a life and the romantic certainty, in spite of my deep skepticism about such things as romance and coincidence, that our lives together were fated by some inexorable and ahistorical force called love.

Love as Escape

Love, of course, is culturally constructed. There is little or no indication that what we describe and experience as romantic love in the Middle Ages, the nineteenth century, or as articulated today in my semi-fictional memoir above existed in antiquity. Plato, as we have seen, rejected its madness and the irrational frenzy of love, describing, in one of his most moving dialogues, the *Symposium*, its different manifestations. Instead he argued for a love defined by the embracing of the ideal forms of the good and the beautiful as the rational man's only choice. Ovid, in his *Remedies of Love* recommended fornication as the cure for infatuation. Anything smacking of idealized love was to be rooted out as a form of weakness, and energetic copulation was to be prescribed as an alternative.

By the twelfth century, troubadour poetry and the invention of courtly love created a space for the romantic attachment as a literary idealization of feeling. Subversive in nature, courtly ideals were a not-so-veiled attack on the institutions and values of the feudal world. As noted earlier, in Gottfried von Strassburg's *Tristan*, the lovers seek refuge in the wilderness, and in the solitude of the cave of crystal, the author's imagined alternative to the Church. Salvation and redemption is to be found in such love. This feeling is not just the ascetic and unfulfilling love from afar, but also the complete union of bodies and minds. This total union, far superior to the mystical renunciation of earthly love for god's love, places the lover outside the bounds of normal society. That courtly love was most often an adulterous affair added a welcome frisson to the undermining of traditional social values. That the betrayal was often at the expense of a well-beloved mentor or lord, or uncle (as in the case of *Tristan*), transgressing loyalty, religion, honor, kinship and friendship further enhanced its subversive nature. Thus, Tristan and Isolde betray their uncle and husband Mark respectively. Guinevere abandons her upright and courtly husband and gives herself completely to Lancelot, Arthur's vassal. Such examples are found again and again in both fiction and histories in the twelfth and in the twenty-first centuries. Couples, moved by love and desire, abandon, at least temporarily, the rules of everyday life. They in fact go away from the normal even if they do not physically move. Not unlike Elvira Madigan (see below and chapter 4), they flee others, finding, even if it is only short-lived as was the case for Tristan and Isolde and Guinevere and Lancelot, a world that contains only the two lovers, who become, not unlike the mystics in their relation to the godhead, one. Within that one, history ceases, time stops. The eternal enemy is conquered howsoever fleetingly.

Nature, often the deep and forbidden forest, and solitude provide an escape for lovers, even if their love is utterly unrequited. In Chrétien de Troyes' delightful story "The Knight with the Lion," the hero Yvain becomes for a short while part of wild nature, abandons his humanness to enter an alternate world, giving himself to the grief of his lost love. In Victor Hugo's *The Toilers of the Sea*, one of those romantic novels that most deeply shaped my adolescence, the protagonist Gilliatt undergoes the most inhumane trials as proof of his love for the unresponsive Deruchette. When the latter leaves with someone else, in spite of Gilliatt's extraordinary sacrifices for her and her father, the forlorn lover sits on a rock, watching the ship that carries her and her husband away from him, as the ocean tide slowly creeps up his body and drowns him. Gilliatt's suicide, the ultimate Camusean statement of our rejection of the world as is, is a commonplace in fiction—think, once again, of Goethe's *The Sorrows of Young Werther*—and, sadly enough, in reality.

I remember well a minor Swedish movie, made memorable because it was animated by Mozart's glorious music. It was entitled *Elvira Madigan* (a movie I revisit in detail in the next chapter), and although I saw it more than four decades ago, the movie still resonates in my mind. The story is an old and tried one. Two young lovers abandon their respective families and flee into summer-lit woods. There, not unlike Tristan and Isolde or the protagonists of *In the Realm of the Senses*, they create an utopian world of love, hunting and gathering fruits as men and women did before property and civilization came along to complicate matters. Their amorous world, in which neither history, family, nor work intrudes, begins to come apart with approaching winter. Compelled by necessity to return to the "world," they choose instead to kill each other, as dying is preferable to giving up their romanticized existence. Again, fiction imitates life. But all these examples tell us of the way in which love, romantic and sexual joined together as one, serves as a powerful means of erasing time and history, even if only ephemerally.

Romantic love, by its very nature, involves at most two or three individuals in its snare. Communal love, when it has been tried—in utopian experimental communities in nineteenth-century America, in the millennium experiments of sixteenth-century Germany, or in the 1960s communal love movement—proves difficult to organize. Our nasty tendency to hold and attempt to own those we love always interferes with the free flow of love. Rather than attempt to describe such perilous enterprises, it may be more useful to explore them from the point of view of the body.

Passion and Sexuality as Escapes
from History and the Self

One does not need Freud to recognize the role that sexuality and the body play in history and in the fleeing from it. From antiquity to the present humans have often lost themselves in the pleasures of the body. The Dionysian pull, so enchantingly described by Nietzsche, was not restricted to the Classical world but remains a constant in our own revelries. Intoxication and the "madness of sexual frenzy," to invoke Plato once more, serve not only to offer a palliative to the miseries of everyday life, but, most of all, to obliterate the self and all its historical implications. Sexual pleasure and the satisfaction of the body offer an alternate way of organizing one's life outside the usual norms of social organization.

Western thought crawls with utopias and dystopias that use sensuality, or even sexuality, explicitly as panaceas for the injustices and cruelties of the world. In some specific cases, the attempt is to abolish the terror of history altogether. In two fairly contemporary and influential, works—written, however, in very different keys: one in the ironic mode and the other in a savagely bitter tone—sex plays a unique role. Aldous Huxley's brilliantly satirical *Brave New World* posits a society in which conditioning, biological selection, and the unlimited pursuit of bodily pleasure provide the answer to how we can be happy while ending the devolution of history. Although there are exceptions (social and intellectual "misfits" safely restricted to an island, "savages" isolated on their "barbaric" reservations, and the all-knowing controllers), a society of consumption, bodily pleasure, and easy access to drugs (combined with biological determinants to happiness) erase history and all the travails that history has long imposed on humanity. If all men (and women) by nature desire to be happy, as Aristotle so famously argued long ago, then the bizarre arrangements found in *Brave New World* have finally provided a possible solution to that enduring human conundrum of achieving happiness for the greatest number. For indeed everyone in *Brave New World*, as awful as that may sound, with the noted exceptions of savages and misfits, is happy. And, far more important, history, defined as "bunk" very early in the book, has also been eradicated. No change, no history. Life is a timeless present.

In a world in which everyone belongs to everyone else and the slightest hint of depression is swiftly handled by the appropriate dose of soma, the past and the future, the burdens of history are radically eliminated into an endless and ongoing present. The institutions that propel history, often with such dire consequences—the state, the family, inequality, property, and the like—are replaced by the daily delights of sports, pneumatic sex, and drugs. All the restrictions that religion and the state have placed on humanity, such as warnings against having too much fun, too much sex, too many drugs—activities that would either lead us straight to hell or, at least, weaken the power of the state—are turned upside down. By authorities ranging from the prophets of the Old Testament to Christian preachers to conservative politicians in twenty-first-century America, we have been told, and continue to be told, that we must never yield to the appetites of the body. Doing so, as Pico della Mirandola argued in his famous *Oration on the Dignity of Man*, would make us the equals of animals. But the citizens of Florence who answered the onslaught of the plague by good old-fashioned debauchery were on to something simple and appealing.

I fear that we are all too well conditioned by religion, ethics, ideals of romantic love, and other such constructs not to be deeply disturbed and even repelled by Huxley's tongue-

in-cheek proposition, though it also functions as a caution-
ary tale, for we are closer to a society like the one depicted in
Brave New World than we might imagine. But, once again, if
the main aim of humanity is to be happy, and if Freud's argument that the most intense and enduring forms of happiness
are sensual ones; then we must pause for a minute and take
Huxley's formulation in all seriousness.

Such utopians as the influential Charles Fourier and Restif de la Bretonne (the latter author of a pornographic semi-
autobiography, *The Anti-Justine*) proposed armies of expert
pleasure-givers, to cure jilted lovers of their forlorn lives.
Restif de la Bretonne envisioned sexual rewards as the means
to improve productivity and strengthen social bonds in the
bourgeoning factories of nineteenth-century Europe. Huxley's unrestricted sexual liaisons, denuded of any moral constraints or romantic possessiveness, seem to me a very pri-
mordial and yet sophisticated answer to the terror of history.
If I am allowed to digress here, I, who as you have seen before
cannot, and will never, escape my romantic upbringing, derive a special pleasure when I read that yet another one of
those conservative paladins of public morality has been caught
in flagrante delicto and that his pious condemnations of sex,
especially of same-gender sex, and bodily pleasures are nothing but a cover for his own unconquerable sexual proclivities.
In many respects, as I noted earlier, sex is one of the most
subversive forces in history, always undermining order, propriety, and other such paragons. If civilization, as Freud argued, is our revenge on the id, we sublimate our desires, ahistorical as they may be, by paying the terrible price of neurosis
and discontent. It seems then that either we give ourselves
entirely to our passions and live a life close to that of the idealized prelapsarian humans, or we live in history and thus
in pain. As Dylan (Bob Dylan) sang in the sixties, "There are

no sins beyond the gates of Eden," that imaginary garden of earthy delights without any of Hieronymus Bosch's nasty punishments at the end.

The other great twentieth-century dystopia is of course George Orwell's 1984. This devastating and prescient book displays sex in a very different fashion. I have already referred to the book and to the place of the proles in its narrative architecture. In this grey and oppressive world, the two main protagonists, Winston Smith and Julia, escape Big Brother's rigid rules and continual manipulation of the past—which is after all what history is: a continuous reshaping of changeable pasts—by the act of copulation. It is not "making love," though Winston and Julia grow quite tender towards each other in the end, it is having sex. When Winston asks Julia whether she has had sex with other party members, and she answers in the positive, adding that she has had such affairs with many, Winston is exhilarated. The more the merrier, for sexuality corrupts and undermines the very fabric of society and, by implication, of history. It is by means of Winston's sexual life, whether in the transgressive and intrinsically repulsive episode with a prostitute, or in his long liaison with Julia, that he physically articulates a long life of thought crimes and resistance to the state. Strangely enough, it is also Orwell, who in his moving *Homage to Catalonia*, peeks briefly into an egalitarian utopian paradise. Stuck in the trenches in a mindless and bloody war, Orwell reflects on the sense of equality, the beginnings of true socialism, with no bosses, no differences, no hierarchy that is found among the Anarchist and P.O.U.M militias on the Huesca front. The horror of *1984* has to be placed side-by-side with the brief glimmer of hope in *Homage to Catalonia* and the possibility of doing away with all those burdens of history: class warfare, inequality, and the like that make for injustice and suffering.

Before Huxley and Orwell, there was of course the Marquis de Sade. In most of his work, but most powerfully in his horrific *120 Days of Sodom*, de Sade presents the reader with a hallucinatory and violent sexual dystopia. As Simone de Beauvoir wrote in her introduction to the book, "Sade made of his eroticism the meaning and expression of his whole existence."[4] As we know from the details of his life, his "sexual idiosyncrasies," to quote de Beauvoir again, were not just contrived literary experiences but part of his life pattern. That is, that while he never really approached the harsh levels of his literary descriptions, de Sade made every attempt to fulfill his fantasies in real life.

In *120 Days of Sodom*, de Sade's four libertines, a word rich in its dual late eighteenth-century meanings of sexual excess and philosophical dissent, gather an army of male and female prostitutes, pimps, elderly storytellers, children of both sexes, and others in a secluded castle, where all sorts of cruelty and sexual transgressions are to be perpetrated on pliant victims, with sodomy, coprophagy, and incomprehensible torture only the high (or low) points within elaborate rituals of sexual and physical abuse. De Sade's book, alarming as it is and repulsive in its cold retelling of the ultimate cruelties that could be inflicted by humans on other humans, offers the author and his readers an alternate understanding of the world and of history. De Sade was, after all, deeply imbricated in his world: caught in the revolutionary upheavals of late eighteenth-century France, a prisoner in the Bastille, and an inmate at the Charenton mental asylum during Napoleon's rule. In the midst of his adversities, he wrote. One may argue that Huxley, Orwell, and de Sade wrote to escape the

---

[4] The Marquis de Sade, *The 120 Days of Sodom and Other Writings*, intro. Simone de Beauvoir and Pierre Klossowski (New York: Grove Press, 1966) 19.

world; that is, that they sought, as Boccaccio did, an aesthetic escape rather than a true embracing of the material world. This would be so were it not that de Sade, as previously noted, although never reaching in his personal life the sheer excesses that he describes in his writing, sought to comes as close as it was possible to do before running afoul of the law. In the flesh, in its pain, its corruption, its sexual deconstruction of bodily excesses carried to the extreme ultimate logical place, that is, dismemberment and death, de Sade and others found an escape from the world and history.

In many senses, de Sade's life and writings stand in sharp contrast to myriads of Western utopias and dystopias in which sexuality in one way or another stands at the center of elaborate ways of escaping or reshaping history. Late nineteenth-century America witnessed a remarkable proliferation of utopian communities. These were not literary or philosophical discussions reserved for the pages of popular books such as Edward Bellamy's *Looking Backward: 2000–1887*, one of the great best sellers of the period, but actual living communities. Intellectually, they all harkened back to Plato's Republic. The latter, far from de Sade's world of physical pleasure and pain, was a well-thought-out attempt to erase family and property, the two main locomotives or institutions of historical change. The aim of the *Republic* was not only to foster the rational life but also to stop change, to end that endless devolution of power that was the source of strife. Communal marriages, an austere and very much controlled and scripted "everyone belongs to everyone else," were not intended for pleasure but for procreation and to undermine the family's ambitions and greed. The point here of course is to notice the extent of the role played by sexual intercourse, the most salient and poignant of all the ways of embracing of the world of matter, in all these formulations of societies outside of history.

Sexuality can also work in a negative sense. Asceticism, most forcefully articulated through celibacy, was at the core of early Christian communities, waiting anxiously for the end of history and the world. In nineteenth-century American experimental societies organized around the denial or experience of sex and, thus, outside the bounds of normative institutions and history (whether rejecting the flesh or embracing it), sex played a central role. The Shakers, a deeply Christian group, rejected any form of sexuality, while living in a communal setting as a way toward salvation. The most interesting experiment, however, was that of the Oneida Society in mid nineteenth-century central New York. Founded in 1848 by John Humphrey Noyes, the Society was in principle a millennial group, but one that affirmed the possibility of perfection and freedom from sin in this world.

Borrowing utopian ideas about sexuality and property from Plato, More, and the whole scientific utopian early-nineteenth-century tradition, Oneida citizens held all property in common and had complex forms of sexual liaisons in which every male was married to every female. Since men were expected not to ejaculate during intercourse, frequent sexual intercourse was at the very center of the society. Older postmenopausal women introduced young men to sex pleasures and mechanics. And since the Oneida community was fairly prosperous, one could see why the outside world could not abide its members' unusual sexual practices and family arrangements. By 1881, two years after Noyes had fled the country to avoid prosecution, the community dissolved.

For our purposes here, this short account of the Oneida experiment, one that has been widely imitated, points to the role that the body, and the body's pleasures, play in formulating ways to escape history. Central to the experience of the 1960s was the liberating feeling that the sexual taboos and restrictions of middle-class America were to be overturned, and that through pleasure, one could also overturn the established order. Of course, what I have been discussing here about sexuality applies equally to drinking, eating, and other forms of sensory gratification. These sensations are part and parcel of our daily existence. It is when they become central to our individual and communal way of seeing ourselves in the world, however, that we step onto a different plane and reject our role as historical agents. In revelry, intoxication, Rabelaisian feasting, and sexuality, many humans have redrawn the terms of their membership in human society and have escaped the burdens of plague, wars, and family obligations. And here one should not end without noting what almost three thousand years or more of religion and "civilization" has done to sexuality in the West. In *The Epic of Gilgamesh*, most likely the first literary text in the history of humanity, Enkidu, the natural man made by the gods to oppose Gilgamesh and who then turns into his devoted friend, becomes "human," by which the epic meant "civilized," as the result of an entire week of energetic copulation with a temple prostitute. What once civilized us, it is now a form of escape from civilization.

Those citizens of Florence who embraced the material world and pleasure as their city crumbled into sickness and ruin did something that other men and women have done and will continue to do through time. For them, the embracing of the world of matter was better than mystical escapes into oneness with the godhead. It was better than religion, and almost always far more pleasurable.

❈IV❈

THE LURE OF BEAUTY AND KNOWLEDGE

IN HIS SOMBER AND oftentimes poignant novel, *Eyeless in Gaza* (1936), Aldous Huxley did not fail to include those mordant commentaries and brilliant asides that illuminated so many of his works. Unexpectedly, in the middle of his plot, Huxley offers the reader a biting appraisal of the scholarly life. His half-humorous, half-sad interpolation into the novel's complex narrative does not take more than a page and a half in the printed edition of the book, but such is its intellectual impact and impeccable dissection of the issues raised here that it may well serve to launch this chapter. Glossing a scholarly statement, "Put four hours on my notes. Extraordinary pleasure," Huxley proceeds to debunk one common way of keeping the burdens of history at bay, namely through scholarship and withdrawal from the world. Or, if I may indulge in an appropriate ironic remark, in the efforts to write this book. A monastic life, a life of celibacy, does not allow, at least in theory, for the physical pleasures that are so vital for human happiness, or so does Huxley argue. Rejection of the world may provide some solace and future heavenly rewards in the afterlife, but that promised, and thus postponed, spiritual delight is bought at the heavy price of sensual deprivation.

Embracing of the material world through the excesses of the flesh and the possession of goods (the theme of chapter 3) remains Huxley tells us, essentially unsatisfying. There is a limit to how much one can drink or eat without serious health penalties. The physical and psychological consequences of a prolonged or continuous state of intoxication are real enough. They are in fact grievous in the end. The same could be said of lovemaking, which is only fully delectable in cycles of denial and fulfillment. As to possessions, the acquisitive soul can never have enough to guarantee happiness. How many paintings and books can one acquire without yearning for the many one cannot ever have, or running out of space to display one's paintings? The latter, by the way, is my own quandary.

Against these dead-end paths to happiness and to the obliteration of grief, Huxley, tongue-in-cheek as we have seen him do in *Brave New World*, presents the life of the scholar— a woman or man who makes and finds meaning in her/his research and writing. And, thus, Huxley's ironic statement, "Four hours at my notes. Extraordinary pleasure," a panacea for the anxieties present in daily existence and in our individual and collective roles as historical agents. Unlike the monk, the glutton, the sex-obsessed individual, or the perpetually drunk, the scholar can have his/her cake and eat it too. He or she can have the aesthetic escape of intellectual work—though I must also admit that physical work is as effective—and the satisfaction on top of that of believing that one is advancing knowledge. All these satisfactions without giving up sex or a stiff drink at appropriate times of the day, or even going on a binge from time to time. One can have scholarship and sex. One may have all the pleasures of the monastery without renunciation, a bit of the pleasures of the flesh, the bottle, and the table, with in addition a veneer of the beautiful and the strong sense of meaning that attaches to one's scholarly or aesthetic pursuits.

Huxley of course was making fun of the scholar. And he was right in doing so. Underneath his satirical/ironical aside lies the shadow that, in far more pages and a far less elegant fashion, I have attempted to outline in this and previous chapters. In the end, whether we choose the "high" road of scholarship and artistic endeavors—high lifers Huxley calls us in derisive tone—or the so-called low road of physical intoxication, or the supposedly even higher road of surrender to the godhead, at the very heart of the quest is an unrequited desire to break away from the invisible chains that tie us to history. The image that comes to mind is that of humanity as a collective Atreus, tied to a rock while birds of prey—history and time—continuously devour its intestines. That was Atreus' punishment for insulting the gods. Not a pretty picture I would say, or a hopeful one, but I fear quite an accurate reflection of things as they are.

As we have seen, in the *Decameron*, after detailing the horrors sweeping Florence in 1348 and the diverse responses of its citizens—either a religious escape or material ones—Boccaccio follows this somber introduction by telling us piquant stories. His protagonists flee the city and its troubles. They entertain each other in a secluded location away from the pestilence by telling and listening to obscene and delightful stories. This is not unlike the Marquis de Sade's horrifying *120 Days of Sodom,* but in a very different key. Boccaccio, the narrator, faced the horror of mid-fourteenth-century Florence by aestheticizing the experience. Not unlike Huxley's imaginary scholar, he put in four hours at his notes. He wrote. He sought to make sense of the horror and to deny it by creating the beautiful.

In one of the most insightful surviving sections of the *Epic of Gilgamesh*, the eponymous protagonist is tormented, after the death of his companion Enkidu, by the realization that he must also die. Enkidu had come in the end to terms with his own mortality. After an angry period of bemoaning having been born, he found redemption and acceptance in his having experienced the benefits of civilization. Gilgamesh refuses to accept death and goes on a long journey in search of immortality. He fails to achieve his goal, and the epic poem ends with the hero at the gates of his city, Uruk, where he sees in tablets carved in a lapis lazuli monument, the rendering into words of all his heroic deeds and accomplishments. Thus, in memory, he finds acceptance for his own inexorable death. How extraordinary that the very first literary work in our collective history deals, first and foremost, with human awareness of the passing of time and our inability to escape death. Remarkably, our insights on these matters have remained fairly constant throughout human existence, even though, as Gilgamesh did, we still seek to escape time and death.

Reading Boccaccio and the *Epic of Gilgamesh* among the many literary works that address these topics, I am continuously in awe of the variety and intensity of human responses to catastrophes—the greatest individual catastrophe being the passing of time—and the manner in which we articulate these responses within a narrow range of ways. These responses come often in a hierarchical order. What I mean by this is that those who command the power of writing, with some notable exceptions—de Sade being one—privilege their own experiences, that is, those of the mind, over their sensory experiences. In many ways, this echoes Freud's definition of "civilization" as a continuous sublimation of one's instinctual and destructive inner core. Yet, as noted in an earlier chapter, the civilizing project may run counter to our basic drives for pleasure, and it is, in its essence, a deterrent to happiness. That is, if we are most happy when we abandon ourselves to the pleasures of the flesh, then when we create art or write history, we are neglecting real pleasure, real happiness in favor of culturally constructed alternatives to sensory pleasures. Yet, here we have a select group of people: philosophers, artists, aesthetes, and other such types of "high lifers" who tell us through their works and writings that they have, not unlike the mystic, found their way to the truth (whatever that may be) and, sometimes, even to happiness. The creative soul can even overcome the most ghastly of catastrophes or the harshest historical events. The impulse to aestheticize the world as we found it—to borrow, once again, the title of Bruce Duffy's very impressive first novel, *The World as I Found It* (1987)—is a most extraordinary act of rendering the horrible into the beautiful (for both Wittgenstein and for Duffy), altering the terror of history through art.[1]

Throughout history, we have been told repeatedly that great art, insightful novels, moving music, emerge most often from the artist's own sufferings. Although this commonplace is of course not universally true, examples of tormented souls who turn their angst into art are numerous enough to make us ponder the kernel of truth present in the assertion. I do imagine that one could list some so-called happy people who still can paint, compose, or write works of beauty, but the giant, the Nietzschian *Übermensch*, is often the man or woman who lives outside the usual norms of society and even of history.

---

[1] Bruce M. Duffy's novel, *The World as I Found It* (New York: Ticknor and Fields, 1987), a fictionalized life of Ludwig Wittgenstein, is a very good example of the manner in which philosophy and art allow a man (Wittgenstein) to deal with his very troubled life, while at the same time Duffy, through his fictionalized account, renders the disasters of history and passing time understandable.

André Schwartz-Bart, a French-Jewish writer whose parents were deported to Auschwitz, confronts in a moving book, *The Last of the Just* (1959), one of the most horrifying events in Western history, the Holocaust. While in the end denying god as an explanation for these horrible acts or even denying god's existence, Schwartz-Bart faces the Shoah by rendering it into art. Through the fictional story of a few just men who by their righteous behavior, love of god, and pain allow the world to survive, Schwartz-Bart provides a somber tale that shifts responsibility from god to humankind. He is not alone in doing so. Others have sought to deal with the horrific events of the Holocaust through literary representations, scholarship, or art, artistic and scholarly contributions that engage in fierce polemics as to the very nature of the carnage. Some, a diminishing number it seems, see the Holocaust as an unprecedented ahistorical moment in mankind's long and troubled story. Others persuasively insist that the Holocaust, with its systematic and cold formal extermination of millions of Jews, Roma, Eastern Europeans, the disabled, Communists, and other marginal people, is just one more chapter in the long history of massacres and genocides that punctuate human history. The horrors of the Holocaust have been somewhat replayed, though at a different scale and for different purposes, in Cambodia, Bosnia, Darfur, and elsewhere. Historians and scholars therefore have sought to trace the historical roots of the Holocaust, looking into old histories of persecution, anti-Semitism, and scapegoating in Western history, attempting to provide an explanation for something that remains the nadir of humanity's long and troubled history.

I am concerned here with art. In providing aesthetic answers to such catastrophes—for other writers have also documented and aestheticized not just the Nazi Holocaust but the Armenian, Cambodian, Rwandan genocides, and other such massacres—novelists, sculptors, and filmmakers have sought to do what seems, at times, a contradictory enterprise. By telling the story through different artistic or scholarly means, they have engaged in a dogged attempt to place these extraordinary acts of inhumanity on record and to identify them as acts of human history. There are of course cases when turning horror into art results in very bad art, nor is exploitation unknown—the turning of horror into art for financial gain. But at its best, the act of writing, painting, composing, or making films about the dark events in mankind's history can offer redemption and catharsis.

If we turn from these unprecedented human catastrophes and horrible historical events and examine instead the individual and the quotidian, we encounter responses that are often focused on the self. This can be done at a very personal level, hidden from the eyes of the world, and for no other purpose than to express one's angst, despair, anger, and frustration. Kafka, writing in the anonymity of his confining job, Céline, with his extreme hostility toward of the world around him, and other similar writers provide numerous examples of creative (and tormented) minds, producing art or something like art as a form of therapy, and, far more important, as a way of resisting the existential and historical contexts of their individual lives. Although Kafka and Céline, to continue with the two examples I have just given, wrote from the perspective of their own individual experiences of historical events, their art allowed them not only to respond to these events but to flee from them as well.

As I mentioned before, during a very dark period in my life between 1978 and 1989 and under the advice of my therapist, I tried to write one very short story every year. I thought about what to write for months and then, sometime in early

135

December, I wrote five to ten pages of things that were often personal and painful. I never revised these stories, sharing them only with a few very close friends. The stories addressed some particular aspect of my life and longings. Two of them, the most sentimental, are included in previous chapters. Often, I could not write what I intended because the experience I wished to convey proved to be still too raw and painful. Such was the case, as I noted earlier, of the story in which I sought to tell the details and experience of my father's death. Even twenty years after his death, I had difficulties doing so, and twice I replaced the story I had originally intended to tell with a short, half-humorous skit. Until one day when, without thinking too much about it, the story poured out of me effortlessly. In many respects, if I survived psychically those years, it was partly because of my ability to exorcize my angst through writing and through my own scholarly work as well. That is, I escaped by "putting in four hours on my notes."

Now, I am, unfortunately, not Franz Kafka in terms of talent and very fortunately not Louis Ferdinand Céline, I hope, in terms of my political leanings. I have none of their talents and none of their politics. But for both the greater and lesser lights in the literary universe, the art of creating, or as pointed out at the beginning of this chapter, scholarship, allows those engaged in the process to temporarily escape the grip of history, even though prompted into their art by history itself. In doing so, the artist or the scholar is able to create an inner world. So for that matter, as rudimentary as they may be, do these pages in front of you.

The artist or maker of culture, more often than not, does not write or create art for himself or herself. Her/his passionate engagement with a subject or artistic theme represents an attempt to reach out beyond the self and to bind readers, listeners, or viewers into a community of insights, a community of beauty, and even a community of suffering. Although we do not always get or understand fully what the artist means to convey, the purpose of all art, it seems to me, is to say something which in its intensity, beauty, horror, or specific themes touches, moves, and changes the observer in a fashion somewhat parallel to the manner in which it changed the creator of that art at the moment of artistic genesis. This is, I think, what great art does and continues to do through time. In his/her work, the artist erases time and death and lives beyond the normal scope of his life. I often tell my students, when showing them a work of art or a movie, or when asking them to read a particular text, that even though the artists may have been dead for many centuries, they are as alive today as they were when they wrote, painted, or created these works. Of course, what I mean is that they are alive in me and other people through the aesthetic response elicited by their works.

How deeply art can touch all of us is a commonplace I need not explain here. All of you who read these pages have your own remembrances of the novel that woke you to the understanding of things, to new experiences and ways of being in the world. You all know the experience of reading something that confirms what you have always known but have not been able to articulate as clearly or as powerfully as the gifted writer you have just read. Similarly, music can take us out of ourselves not just as an emotional and sensual release—as described, for example, in an earlier chapter in reference to the experience of the rave—but as a deep and moving aesthetic experience, as a thing of beauty beyond reason or hope. Lynn Hunt, a great historian of the French revolution and, very fortunately for me, a colleague and friend, has recently argued that the rise of human rights in the West was directly linked to the reading of epistolary novels in the eighteenth century. Novels gave access to subjectivity and to the understanding that other human beings were like one's self. That subjectivity, gained through art and literature, is both a path into and out of history.

In a strange and unforgettable fashion, I can date to the hour and minute the moment I ceased to be an adolescent, though to be perfectly honest I am sure that many of my colleagues and friends would argue that I have never really ceased to be one. The moment, an aesthetic experience but a powerful emotional one as well, occurred while watching François Truffaut's debut New Wave film, *The Four Hundred Blows* (*Les quatre cents coups*, 1959). I was still very much an adolescent, barely sixteen, and the movie, which in fact had no resonance with my own life at all, imprinted my consciousness for the rest of my life. It was perhaps the iconic ending with the teenager escaping the reformatory where he had been placed by an uncaring and adulterous mother and catching his first glimpse of the sea, our primeval mother. Whatever it was, I will remember it for as long as I live, or until my mind plays the ultimate cruel trick on me by involuntarily removing me from history and time through dementia or total forgetfulness. Until then, Truffaut lives in me, as do other writers, painters, composers, and film makers.

Are they not, these aesthetic epiphanies, also a form of escaping history, of removing oneself from the weight of time and the burden of history? Again, not every artist seeks to achieve these transcendental moments, but some do, and they take us with them into another world of experiences. If we enter their world and make it our own, then we are continuously engaged with the dead. They are all around us, pointing to us a new way to follow, transforming our lives. A very talented and young Anglo-Indian writer, Jhumpa Lahiri, in her second work, *The Namesake*, (her first full novel after her impressive collection of short stories entitled *The Interpreter of Maladies*), tells a complex story about the difficulties of living in two cultures, the joys and pains of family obligations, love, relations, and betrayal. What moved me to tears in a novel in which the emotional register did not always rise to the very high level of her previous work or to her recent collection of short stories was her last sentence. The protagonist opens a novel by his namesake Gogol and begins to read, right after his father's death. The author provides a most powerful and unexpected conclusion to her work, while tying up the different strands of her narrative. In doing so, she delivers an insightful reminder of what books and reading mean and the special place they hold in the long list of ways in which we escape the daily horrors of existence and personal tragedies. Here again the protagonist of Lahiri's *The Namesake*, by reading Gogol (his father's favorite author and a book that had saved his father's life), reconnects with the enduring line that links us to others through the lure of the beautiful.

Recently, I taught a class on world history from the Big Bang to around 400 CE. As I do in all my classes—something that I first did as a teaching assistant to the blessed Carl Schorske at Princeton almost four decades ago—I gave the students the choice of performing in lieu of one of the papers. The performances could range from music, dance, dramatic representations, or any other creative form of connecting themselves and their act of learning with the past. I have seen some very memorable performances and some utterly horrible ones over the years. Probably because the class had a large number of freshmen, few took the opportunity of performing in front of their classmates. We only had three performances. All three were excellent. The first was a musical performance based upon the *Odyssey*, involving some elaborate and complex original music played on an electric guitar.

The second was an energetic and spirited rendition of a Garba Raas, a traditional Indian dance from Gujarat usually performed at the festival of Navratri. It was also engaging and moving. But it was the last performance that was transformative. Two young students, a young man and a young woman, played the guitar and violin and sang verses from the *Bhagavad Gita* to music that the young woman had composed. When they concluded their performance, the students in the class, more than three hundred of them, stood up and gave them an ovation. Some had tears in their eyes. I did too. I was speechless in this moment that was transcendental, not in a religious sense but in an aesthetic one. In this moment, a moment out of time, as I listened and saw them perform, there was nothing outside the music. I was, and many of my students were, outside history and time. So were the performers who had captured in a fleeting, temporal sense, a bit of something beyond the self. Yet, there was also sadness. For me there was certainly a sense of emptiness at the ephemeral nature of the emotion, at seeing and understanding something that could not be captured or felt the same way ever again. That one had to return to the here and now, while, in another plane, one lived in beauty. I think my students also shared in that sense of having seen something special happen all around them, and yet, something that could not be retained as a protection against the passing of time, but had to be kept like a charm or protective amulet in memory. Of course, they both received an A+.

In a sense, books, as do art, music, scholarship and other cultural forms of making meaning, work at two distinct levels. They are often, though not always, the artist or scholar's working out of his or her individual complex set of emotions and expectations. These experiences and the telling of them do not always seek to transform others. Rather, they probably aim at a self-transformation, though the hope of touching others is always implicit in the process of creating the beautiful and in the act of sharing it. At a second level, art transforms not just the artist but others as well, providing, as described above, that moment of release from the quotidian. Speaking of my own experiences, books—far more than music or visual art, for the experience that I related above is an exception—have always been a refuge for me. Even as a child, I fled my friends and family, took a book with me, usually (depending on how old I was) Jules Verne, Emilio Salgari's novels of Sandokan and his band of fellow pirates, Alexandre Dumas, Victor Hugo, or Sir Walter Scott, and spent most of the day alone, lying on a stone table or on the grass in a remote corner of Ernest Hemingway's farm (which was located right across the street from my own home in Cuba).

In my early teens, I did not experience many great catastrophes, except for the death of a younger sister after months of illness, to flee from. Nor did I meet family conflicts or all those other myriads of terrible things that may turn childhood or adolescence into veritable nightmares. All to the contrary, my life was relatively well ordered, loving, and free of great stress. But having read all those impossibly romantic nineteenth-century novels, I was a peculiar adolescent, suffering (or so I proudly and misguidedly thought at the time) from that peculiar illness of the sensitive young: *Weltschmerz*, a melancholy of the world. It led to a sense of alienation, of being different, that was, contradictorily, comforting and painful at the same time. Again, I know that I write here about something quite common. Many of the young students I have taught over almost four decades have hinted at such distress or fully articulated it, even though they have not read or known anything about nineteenth-century romantic novels. In spite of my experience, romantic novels may not be the only catalyst for to such experiences of an uncomfortable sense of difference.

The point here of course is that all these symptoms that I have described do not necessarily qualify fully as attempts to escape history. Nonetheless, they all have the potential for shutting out the world and the quotidian. When I fled to my quiet corner and read, I was never alone or in the present. Athos, Aramis, Porthos, and d'Artagnan were with me, and so were Edmond Dantès, Chicot, Gilbert, Esmeralda, and an entire cast of fictional characters who were, and still are, as real to me as the world outside. Having seen the film, as well as read the book upon which the film is based, of Jean-Dominique Bauby's tragic life and death, *The Diving Bell and the Butterfly*, I have been powerfully and emotionally reminded of the truth in John Donne's often quoted sermon that "no man is an island entire of itself" and that every death diminishes us. Tragedies, whether as widespread and devastating as the Black Death proved to be for mid-fourteenth-century Europe, or the recent killings in Darfur, or the ongoing drug cartel massacres in Mexico, or even individual tragedies, such as Bauby's, all of them have a way of reminding us of our own mortality and, often, allowing us to identify with the horrors of epidemics, famines, war, or individual suffering.

The victim of a massive cardiovascular stroke, Bauby ended up in the rare but exceedingly cruel condition called the "locked-in syndrome." Though able to think with astonishing clarity and to hear and see (though his sight was limited to one eye) things around his bed, he could only articulate his thoughts by blinking his one still-functioning eye. It was in this way that he dictated the book to his secretary. Bauby could not help but draw a parallel between himself and Nortier, one of Dumas' most extraordinary characters in

The Count of Monte Cristo, who communicated with his beloved granddaughter Valentine, by winking. Here, once again, the power of literature transcends even the most painful of circumstances. Rather than being a depressing novel or film, Bauby's last work—he died shortly after the book was published—is an exhilarating affirmation of life and of the power of memory and art to overcome a major health catastrophe. Without god, with only the memory of sex (vivid though it was), with no speech, with no sensation, Bauby's mind flew free like the butterfly of the title and escaped the confining prison of his body that he metaphorically describes as a diving bell, or, more accurately, a deep-ocean diving suit. For him, history had stopped. The present, the self became triumphant. His art sought to make one single point: Here I am! I exist!

Utopias

In considering the manifold ways in which we deal with the world, we should note the Western proclivity for imagining and even taking steps to create a perfect world and, of course, in doing so to stop change. We have seen some of these attempts in chapter 2 under the guise of apocalyptic movements that, violently and/or piously, sought to trigger the second coming, the end of time, and the end of history. Philosophers and science fiction writers have also sought to imagine such a world from a purely intellectual and aesthetic perspective. For them—and these utopian writers come in the most amazing variety—change is often the enemy. And is not history and the historical project at its very core the study of change over time? All utopias, or at least *most* utopias are essentially ways to escape history. They emerge from one fundamental premise: that the world is full of injustice and inequality, that historical processes as they have worked throughout time have yielded unbearable social conditions, and that these conditions are not conducive to the happiness of humanity. Thus, the individual cannot be truly happy because he/she cannot be truly just in an unjust world. Plato, the author of the first, and many would argue best, utopian work, the *Republic*, begins precisely with a discussion of what justice is. One of those crossing verbal swords with Plato's protagonist, his mentor Socrates, was the sophist Trasymachus. His views, Machiavellian *avant la lettre*, posit a world in which the will and interests of the strong determine the nature of government and social relations. Is it not precisely this fact that history and the study of history are truly all about?

If we look into our long collective past, what we see again and again are violent clashes between different factions of individuals who seek rulership, control, power, and the ability to impose their own vision—enlightened or nefarious as it may be—on their fellow human beings. And in writing history, more often than not, our efforts are clearly aimed at describing and explaining the workings of power and inequality over time. These were precisely the evils that led Plato—who had seen the awful results of Athenian defeat in the Peloponnesian War and the impact of the plague on Athens—to propose the creation of a society in which strife and change would be eliminated, though he admits to the possibility of his Republic's decline and transformation into an unjust state. He attempts to carry out these ideas—there was an actual experiment at creating such a society in Sicily—by controlling, through a series of underhanded schemes—the evil influences of property, family, and sexuality. The Republic, above all, would allow to the few the liberating contemplation of "the beautiful and the good."

It is true that Plato's *Republic* borrowed heavily from Sparta's model. Plato was fascinated, as were most of his contemporaries, by Sparta's seeming ability to remain unchanged for centuries and by the essential communism, or sharing of property, of its ruling military elite. Sparta's stable and conservative regime had what the Greeks described as *eunomia*, the quality of being well ruled. Although historical reality did differ from the ideal, Plato's *Republic* and Marx's transition to full communism, though deeply grounded in historical realities, were in their full and final destinations implicit rejections of history. In the former, the tripartite division of society into castes of workers, guardians, and philosopher kings, all ruled by reason, would bring to an end the historical devolution of power that led inexorably, as had been the case in Athens, to demagoguery, imperialist ventures, class strife, and eventual defeat. Marx's advanced stages of communism would bring an end to the long history of class antagonisms. It would bring about the omnicompetent man and the final withering away of the state. In both cases, although the means of achieving these ends was deeply imbedded in historical processes, the outcomes were essentially ahistorical and, in a deeper sense, anti-historical. In Plato and Marx, writers who were both passionate and scholarly at the same time, the intellectual response to the vicissitudes of history was an almost visceral reaction to the eternal evils plaguing mankind: inequality, exploitation, and injustice. These common historical categories, present as they are in every system of government throughout time, are at the very heart of the terror of history.

Of course, Plato and Marx are only two of the most notable utopian writers in the history of the West. Ideal futures emerge as responses to many of these issues. Edward Bellamy's *Looking Backward* (published in 1888), an exceedingly popu-

145

lar story and a best seller in late nineteenth-century America, was the catalyst for the actual formation of numerous Bellamy societies. These associations hoped to bring Bellamy's vision to fulfillment. That vision was, most of all, a conservative reaction to industrialization and the evils that the Industrial Revolution had visited upon the Anglo-American world. Bellamy's world, a post-industrial society, had abolished property in favor of a communitarian and highly transcendentally inspired perfect and unchanging world. Charlotte Perkins Gilman's *Herland* (published in 1915), another one of those abundant late-nineteenth-century American utopian dreams, depicted a female-only society in which the historical evils of patriarchy had finally been vanquished and replaced by a matriarchal society (reproducing itself though parthenogenesis) in which wars, property, and abuses of power (mostly by men) were no more.

I could go on listing the numerous utopian societies: both in their idealized versions and in their always unsuccessful (in the long run) attempts at implementation. The patterns are almost always the same. Such formulations are, after all, at their core literary enterprises, seeking to eliminate some well-defined historical evil that is rightly perceived as the root of inequality and unhappiness. I am not interested here in the manner in which these utopias were and are produced, but in the creative or artistic drive that animates them. Not unlike music, sculpture, painting, filmmaking, and literature, utopias address and provide solutions to our quandary of being trapped in history. Also, not unlike these aesthetic expressions, the trajectory is more or less the same: awareness of the terror of history, its rejection, and the formulation, either through a burst of creativity by a single artist or complex collective plans for the betterment of mankind, of a journey to a place beyond history. Unlike the millennial yearnings and outbursts we witnessed earlier, which sought a return to god and an end to time and history, utopias, with some notable exceptions, such as the Shakers, *Christianopolis,* and the Jesuits' utopian experiments in early modern Paraguay, were quite secular in their aims, and, in some cases, devoutly anti-Christian. In fact, utopias and dystopias identified the formal religions of the West as one of the evils plaguing mankind, thus *Brave New World.*

If philosophical salvation and true happiness are to be found in the contemplation of "the beautiful and the good," as in Plato, or in equality and meaningful labor, as in the communism of Marx, then there is little room for a competing belief. True, Plato betrayed himself and all of his readers throughout later centuries with his mysterious and lyrical denouement (The Myth of Er) at the end of the *Republic* and his withdrawal into the Pythagorean transmigration of souls. And Marx's communist and stateless society has all the feel of a secular religion. Yet, their process of deconstructing the histories and structures of their own peculiar times owes nothing to the divine.

Sometimes different literary genres provide surprising clues to an artist's yearnings to escape his/her historical context and to create a different world, whether utopian or dystopian. The examples from science fiction and fantasy literature are many indeed. There is no need here to review many of these works. Some of them are obscure and little known to the general reading public. Others have become part of our culture. Two authors who exemplify the second category are Arthur C. Clarke and Frank Herbert. In his iconic science fiction work, *2001*, so superbly rendered into film by the incomparable Stanley Kubrick, Clarke raises a series of important questions about history and the world to come. Though the respective endings, both of the movie and the novel, remain purposely enigmatic and opaque, it is clear that human history is seen in *2001* from a different perspective. The encounter with the mysterious monolith opens new avenues for mankind's development that are beyond human history. The same occurs in Clarke's provocative and suggestive *Childhood's End*. Mankind, with the exception of a few reluctant humans, joins in a spiritual and transcendental escape from human history into higher forms of consciousness. If one would note the parallels between *Childhood's End* and the Heaven's Gate collective suicide, the similarities, though differently plotted, are disturbing indeed.

The other author I would mention here is the rightly celebrated Frank Herbert. In his *Dune* books—six of them in all—he constructs a society clearly borrowed from the historical model of the Arab expansion after the death of the Prophet Muhammad in 632. His desert planet Arrakis and the all-powerful anti-aging substance called "melange," that could only be found on that planet underpinned a vast galactic empire. So far so good, and in the earlier stages of his massive opus, Herbert keeps very much within the parameters of a fictionalized historical plotting. But by the end of volume 3, *Children of Dune*, and all through volume 4, *God, Emperor of Dune*, Herbert takes a bold step both into fantasy and into having his main protagonist, Leto, engage in what I would call the forcing of history into a static paralysis that denies the possibility of historical processes. For four thousand years, as Leto slowly turns into a sandworm (a gigantic beast that produces the all-necessary melange), he becomes the repository of all human memories and histories. He rules a world in which change and its concomitant twins, progress and decline, are kept under very tight reins. This is the Golden Path, as Herbert describes it, and necessary for saving mankind from itself. Half religion, half conscious attempt to shape a permanent and unchanging future, the Golden Path is also a deeply utopian or dystopian project, an escape from unavoidable wars, struggles for power, patriarchy (Leto's armies are female), and the like, which, in Herbert's formulation, threaten to extinguish the human race.

The Dissolution of the Self

In the endless struggle between self and community, between acquiescing to or escaping from the terrors of history, nothing has proved as dangerous as attempts to obliterate the self. This destruction of the self may come in different guises. It may take the merely physical form of ending one's misery through suicide—an old and well-tried method whether undertaken individually or collectively. It could be an emancipation from the self by means of religious intoxication, a mystical trance, or union with the godhead. The aesthete may also imagine paths that lead to the same outcome. The roads may be those of art, beauty, and knowledge, but the results are the same. I do not mean to imply here that the writer or creative mind can remove himself or herself from the world literally, or that a reader or viewer, that is, a person gazing somewhat vicariously upon art can directly share in that unique state that here, for lack of a better term, I have described as the dissolution of the self. There are, nonetheless, certain forms of artistic expression—writing and film come first to mind—in which the narrative thrust of the work's plotting leads inexorably to a form of escape from time and history. What I seek to describe here is both contained in specific types of works of art, almost nihilistic in their intent, and in the very process of engaging with the beautiful or the abominable.

Of the first, there are many examples worth pursuing, but van Gogh's mounting and disturbing crescendos of colors and his self-centered artistic perception of the world is a fitting example. Even if we did not know of his tragic life, illnesses, and eventual death, his paintings would speak to us powerfully of a sublime, though alarming as well, withdrawal into art as an alternative to the so-called reality of the world outside him. If we are still so fascinated with van Gogh's works almost a century after his death, it is because of the unique intensity of his angst, anger, and despair at life, and because of how those sentiments were conveyed in his art and, thus conveyed to us who gaze on his paintings. Baudelaire's (1821–67) cynical and moving poems and his famous, and already-quoted dictum that one ought to go through life intoxicated, should not, I think, be read as an invitation to take refuge in alcohol and drugs, a path that, as we saw in the previous chapter, many of us remember from the sixties. What Baudelaire urged was, rather, an escape into the intoxication offered by aesthetics, an escape, via poetry, art, music from everyday life, from its misery, horrors, and most of all from its tedium.

There is a line from an anonymous eighteenth-century suicide note that sought to justify the violent ending by the need to put an end, in an age before zippers or Velcro, to "all that buttoning and unbuttoning." As caustic as that formulation is, it contains in its simplicity an extraordinarily sharp insight into the heart of things. The terror of history consists —one must be continuously reminded—of far more than just inexplicable catastrophes or the nadir of man's violence against man and his destructiveness to the planet. The terror of history may also consist of the dreadful absurdities of everyday life, of the oppression of quotidian banalities, of the inexorable passing of time. The mindless repetition of essentially boring activities—the daily buttoning and unbuttoning —the awareness, though it does not have to be always this way, that our lives are essentially plotted for us, all of that can be overwhelming and disturbing. The sense that every morning I will wake up more or less at the same time, follow the same routine in preparing my breakfast, reading the newspapers, and checking my e-mail before sitting down joyfully to my "four hours at my notes" can become, when reflected upon rather than done automatically by rote, a powerful reminder of the futility of our, or in this case, my own existence. In many respects these well established routines, the patterns of everyday life, provide large doses of comfort and security as well. They give us a false sense of an ordered universe. They provide context and meaning to our lives and, in a sense, a fleeting form of happiness as well. These routines can go on for a long time, providing a sense of continuity, linking our individual lives to the past (this is what I do every day) and to the future (this is what I will do tomorrow). In some cases, they provide the contours for an entire existence. There are many, lucky or unlucky, for whom the course of their lives shows little or no departure from these well-ordered routines. As comforting as this may seem, in the end it is also an unspeakable horror.

Yet, I think that if we were able to open a window into the minds of those whose lives move along such well-plotted courses, we might be surprised at the occasional rage that burns inside. That seething anger is never, or seldom, articulated. It is never, or only occasionally, allowed to surface into creative or destructive bursts of activity. That is why sometimes we hear of the suicide or unexpected behavior of someone who, having led a quiet or even exemplary (in its mediocrity) life, suddenly, with little or no sign of his or her intentions, does something completely different from the patterns that had so clearly shaped his or her life. I remember a story I was told by one of my relatives. A grandfather took his grandson to the school-bus stop every morning. One day the child asked his grandfather, "Grandpa, do I have to do this every day of my life? For how long do I have to go to school?" When the grandfather waxed poetic about high school (the child was only in second grade), college, even graduate school, the kid was in total despair, unable to grasp that for the next twenty years or more of his young life he would do just this one thing that occupied most of his time and left so little space to play. "What a boring thing to do," he said.

As we know, from the mouths of children comes great wisdom. In that little anecdote, told to me many years ago by the actual grandfather, we may grasp the heart of the conundrum I have sought to unravel over the last three chapters. We oscillate perilously between the excitement and terror of occasional catastrophic events—though they seem to be too common lately to be called "occasional"—and the tedium of repetitive behavior and predictable lives. Collectively and individually, we flee and/or combat the former; we also flee and/or combat the latter. We have already seen the weapons with which we have armed ourselves to do battle against history and the banal: religion, physical pleasure, and, finally, the pursuing and possessing of the beautiful and of knowledge, or, far more to the point, the creative process itself. In many respects, in spite of my many attempts to refuse to rank these three different responses to the terror of history as one superior to the other, there are significant differences.

Pursuing the beautiful, the making of art as a way of conveying and dealing with the unrest of the heart or the mind or the need to escape some disturbing situation is more often than not an individual exercise. Few societies have existed in which the driving, organizing principle has been the creation and care of beautiful things. It must be of course clearly understood that I do not describe the beautiful here as a Platonic category, that is, as something immutable and absolute. Beauty is always related to taste, and taste is always culturally constructed. Nonetheless, no society has ever pursued aesthetic goals as a whole or allowed all of its citizens to share equally in the benefits of the aesthetic experience. Plato's utopian musings in the *Republic*, a book consciously driven by a hierarchy of forms or ideas in which the ultimate awareness was of "the beautiful and the good," did not in the slightest conceive of a society in which all citizens would be engaged in the contemplative life. Someone had to grow food and clean the toilets! The life of the mind was open only to the very few. A large contingent of workers and guardians was required to underpin the long and arduous journey of the Philosopher King to the contemplation of the Beautiful. Though Plato's sojourn in "the beautiful and the good" in the end smells, as already noted, of mysticism, the steps up the ascending ladder of forms were always the work of reason.

I have wandered, as is often my proclivity, away from the point I have been attempting to make. That is, that we should not be too surprised that the refuge into aesthetics is often thought of as "superior" to the escapes provided by religion and/or intoxication. And of course the creator of art or new knowledge may also enjoy a stiff drink—they often do—sex, and even religion, thus, Huxley's ironic comments glossed at the beginning of this chapter. Ruskin, to cite just one more example, cultivated an aestheticism that was to be placed at the service of religious sensibility. Nonetheless, artists or scholars are often driven, most of all, by their art or research, a form both of religion and intoxication. And the claim is that in pursuing their métier, aesthetes produced (and still create) things—paintings, poetry, novels, films, and the like—that conquer fleeting time, that reach out to generations to come with one powerful message: "Here I am. I endure."

Walking through Paris, a city were the ruling elite and the citizens are perhaps more self-consciously reflective of their own historical past than the people of any other city in the world (though Venice has certainly claims as well), we see civic spaces that have sought to capture beauty through monuments, impressive perspectives, and harmonious architecture. Every year when I visit Paris in the summer, I am always struck by the sheer beauty of the city and by how competing ages overlap, like strident children, clamoring for our attention. In the end, it works because the past, while borrowing from a previous age, always aims for an unknown future; thus, transcending history and its limitations. Paris comes as close as I know—without being yet a museum city à la Venice or simply magnificent ruins à la Angkor-Wat—to embodying this ideal of beauty. One can get lost in the past while still being within a real and thriving modern city. Walking into an impasse off the rue du Faubourg Saint Antoine or strolling on the rue Servandoni off the rue de Vaugirard hurls one unwittingly out of the present and into the past. And that past is neither consciously nor unconsciously a play of memory à la Proust, but one that paradoxically, while grounded and feeding from historical experiences, transcends history itself. If the purpose is always to escape time, above all one's own time, then getting lost in the past, traveling to it by being taken in by the beauty of a street or by reading, is an escape as attractive—or far more so—than a mystical experience. The aesthetic approach is thus harder, more exclusive, more individualistic, and thus less open to those great emotional waves of apocalyptic feelings or revolutionary fervor that have often swept large portions of mankind to resist, and escape from, history. This almost lyrical aestheticism is difficult to explain, more difficult to convey. One must live it directly. Like the mystical experience, the awareness and possession of the beautiful is ineffable.

Cities are, and Paris most of all, engines for historicizing the past and constructing historical contexts for individuals and communities, for citizens and visitors. Yet, when city elites and rulers choose to aestheticize the civic context, the results, when such results are fully or even partially successful, that is, when those organizing space create an artful layering and organizing of the historical past, their efforts both reinforce the sense of an endless cultural borrowing and historical continuity and, as noted earlier, also propose a construct in which different historical patterns and ages are rendered as if existing in the moment and immune to change. We know, of course, how illusory and elusive such an idea is in the end.

In Marcel Proust's concluding paragraphs of *Swann's Way* (*Du côté de chez Swann*) the first volume of his sweeping and moving *À la recherche du temps perdu*, the main protagonist of the entire opus reflects on the mutability and unavoidable flaws of both remembered places and time. Evoking how Madame Swann looked as she walked on the Bois de Boulogne, the narrator compares those who walked the avenues of the Bois in his own time, altering inexorably the actual reality of place: "as ephemeral as time itself." It is, then, in the workings of memory, both as a continuous awareness of things as they were and as they are no more that one grasps the terrible understanding that place and people are as ephemeral as time itself. This is how Proust puts it:

> ... and helped me to understand how paradoxical it is to seek in reality for the pictures that are stored in memory, which must inevitably lose the charm that comes to them from memory itself and from not being apprehended by the senses.

The reality I had known no longer existed. It sufficed that Mme Swann did not appear, in the same attire and at the same moment, for the whole avenue to be altered. The places we have known do not belong only to the world of space on which we map them for our own convenience. They were only a thin slice, held between the contiguous impressions that composed our life at that time; the memory of a particular image is but regret for a particular moment; and houses, roads, avenues are as fugitive, alas, as the years.[2]

Proust's painful awareness of this mutability of things and of the flow of time and memory is the point of departure for his attempt to fix the world and time in an aesthetic reverie. In his particular case, he did so through his monumental and heartrending literary work.

Finally, the aesthetic realization of the transitory nature of all things often leads to a commitment to cultural projects that are essentially at odds with the flowing and impermanent nature of reality. Once again, all art is a struggle against the passing of time. Think, for example, of the meticulous and long-term work necessary for the building of the pyramids. Beyond being resting places and launching points into the life after, the pyramids were built to conquer time and to secure remembrance into a far future. The remarkable thing is that such a struggle, when done well, whether in architecture or literary works, is often successful. Proust, both the author and his protagonist, were reclusive characters. Confronting his ambivalent sexuality, his illnesses, Proust spent most of his life in a personal journey through memory, recovering a particular past through writing. But he also, through

[2] Marcel Proust, *In Search of Lost Time*, vol. I, *Swann's Way*, trans. C. K. Scott Moncrieff and Terence Kilmartin, rev. D. J. Enright (New York: The Modern Library, 1992) 606.

the metonymic and artificial use of fleeting moments, grasped them as keys to aesthetic experiences.[3] Yet, the most devastating (and beautiful) passages in Proust's long and complex work are those same passages in which he comes to terms with the instability of words, places, and time.

Not unlike the mystic or the hedonist, one who attempts to escape the conundrum of the human condition by means of the aesthetic ends often in that dead-end street from which there is no exit. If the artist "succeeds" in creating something that endures through time, the meaning of his or her art changes inexorably, shaped by shifting contexts. If the film *The 400 Blows* moved me and others in peculiar ways more than four decades ago, I doubt very much that it would do the same to those now of the same age I was then. Instead, the movie is often seen as either dated, or as yet another landmark in the history of the cinema. Denuded of its immediacy by changing tastes and by the evolution of films that *The 400 Blows* itself helped propel, the attempt for aesthetic permanence is a failed one. When we turn the beautiful into a scholarly inquiry something fundamental vanishes.

Since I am rereading Proust for reasons that have a great deal to do with my present age (old), my love for things French and Parisian, and a growing awareness—one that I have always had but without the sharpness it possesses today—that life is, after all, meaningless, I am struck again and again by the sheer magnitude of Proust's project of retrieving, reordering, and redeeming his own life through art. I am most of all struck by the unexpected turns of phrase or thought that capture the tragic heart of things in flashes of rhetorical virtuosity and insight. Writing in the context of an unprecedented war

---

[3] Peter Collier, *Proust and Venice* (Cambridge: Cambridge University Press, 1989) 45–47 et passim.

(WWI), rapid social changes, and worldwide crises, Proust's works, written between 1908 and 1922, barely touch or reflect directly some of these important historical transformations or catastrophes. Instead, the works are all about interiority. It is about what Collier describes in his *Venice and Proust*, as a vast project to fold life, sensations, beauty itself, into transcendental beauty. Thus, Swann is fascinated with Odette at first because her face resembles those faces found in Botticelli's paintings. So is Albertine to Marcel, a fleeting vision of a work of art.

If history, as I noted before quoting Ruth MacKay, is the cross we all bear, how much better it is, therefore, to remove that cross from our shoulders. If the very essence of Christianity is that Jesus carried the cross and died on it so that humanity did not have to do so, if intoxication and/or sensual pleasures are ways to suspend, howsoever fleeting these moments may be, the burdens of god(s) and history, then art provides the same kind of relief. It does so for the individual artist or scholar. It does so collectively for those who, always at a risk, enter the world that the aesthetes have created.

As I sit at my computer, churning out one book or article after another, a suspicion gnaws at my mind. Almost like an alarm clock unpleasantly ringing in the morning's early hours, it tells me that, as serious as I am about the reconstruction of the past, both the projects themselves and my seriousness are forms of escape, of erasing meaninglessness. It is all a bit delusional. Does my work really amount to anything? Does it really matter? Does it fulfill any meaningful purpose? Early in my career, it meant tenure, promotion, recognition, but now what? Why, I ask myself, am I doing this when I could be reading Jane Austen or Proust, watching films, being a flâneur in Paris? Were I to take these questions to their logical conclusions and act upon them, I would be moving closer to the answers chosen by the individuals in the previous chapters. Pleasure and dissolution would be my true escape. Were I to recover religion, a kind of Proustian, "time regained," I would be following the lead of those examples presented in chapter 2. The reality is that I do not act on these impulses, or at least not yet. Instead, I write. I write books about festivals. I write things like this. I write short tales for my granddaughter. I read novels. I buy art. I look at my paintings with great relish every day. I love my wife intensely against all odds and the passing of time. I try to surround myself with beauty and friends. I give parties and cook up a storm for my guests. I go to Paris every year. I try to keep the terrors of history outside my door, though they intrude powerfully in the newspapers. They, these dispatches from a world afar and near and almost always bad, are religiously and tediously left outside my door very early in the morning by a faceless worker. This worker is barely scratching out a living. He or she has no time or leisure to think or reflect on the terror of history as a conscious enterprise. The terror of history intrudes in the morning CNN telecasts, in the *Journal* of TV5MONDE. It intrudes in conversations with friends and colleagues. I learn of yet another catastrophe, natural or man-inflicted. I read about and see with my own eyes the growing gap between rich and poor. I read about droughts, floods, earthquakes, and raging fires. I heard last year the strident debates on health insurance and the sheer stupidity, misinformation, prevarication, and malice of some of the participants in that debate. I ponder about deep and dark existential questions, about the meaning of my own life. And then, I write. I read. But the escape is only temporary. The doubts and questions return. There is, in truth, no exit.

I think many artists know this. And they know it with far more clarity than I ever could. Albert Camus comes to mind immediately. They know it as a reflection of their lives and, intuitively, through their works. Nonetheless, the act of creating the beautiful is in its very essence a meaning-making enterprise. That in itself points to an inherent contradiction. While on the one hand most art is an affirmation of life and thus a validation of history; on the other hand the yearning for remembrance and for transcending the flow of time is, above all, an attempt to escape. Of the first, the examples abound. Dostoevsky's joyful ending in *The Brothers Karamazov* is an example of the embracing of life and the reaffirmation of continuity and the flow of time against even the direst of circumstances. Yet, as noted earlier, the book also contains some of the most bitter condemnations of human history in general and of religion in particular as, for example, those ideas rendered so poignantly in the bitter story of the Grand Inquisitor. A world in which humanity chooses bread over freedom, chooses to be told what to do rather than to choose. The tale of the old grand inquisitor in late medieval Toledo is told by Ivan to the believing Alexis. Moreover, there is throughout the book a tone that approaches nihilism. Yet, the book ends with an epiphany in which belief and joy reassert themselves. Religion and history themselves ameliorate mankind's inability to live in freedom.

Of the second path, writings that emphasize the meaninglessness of life and history, Camus' *The Stranger* or Sophocles' lapidary comment "that it is better not to be born," both of them already invoked in the introduction to this book, are naked and direct acknowledgments that life is either meaningless or so burdensome that ending it is the most rational thing one can do. I have already glossed the impact that a Swedish film, *Elvira Madigan*, had on me. It may be useful to revisit it here. In its idyllic beauty—the protagonists, setting, and background music being equally attractive—*Elvira Ma-*

digan is in its first half a utopian dream in which two individuals become one and escape the tedium and burdens of everyday life into a kind of prelapsarian paradise. I think that many of us who saw this film more than forty years ago, did so with envy, wishing for the courage to step out of history and out of our conventional lives. We hoped for the redeeming quality of a return to nature and to a life of love. And in the 1960s, many did just this: populating communes, experimenting with different forms of social organizations and family, with different kinds of sexuality, and following a drug-induced road to higher modes of consciousness.

But if some of us remember this movie so vividly, or as vividly as I do, it was not because of its protagonists' message of abandoning the well-trodden path, but because of its denouement. Summer, as is always the case, gave way to fall, and fall to winter. The ground froze. Fruits that the protagonists had plucked easily from trees were no longer to be found. Flowers died. The unforgiving facts of everyday life came rushing in on the characters. In order to survive, they had to return to the world, face the censure of the communities and families they had left behind in their amorous rapture, return to their oppressive routines of everyday life. As we have already seen, they chose something else. They chose to die. Death was preferable to what they saw as a betrayal of their romantic dreams.

Writing on the wrong side of my sixty-seventh birthday and remembering this story with surprising romantic longings—which does tell a great deal about the fact that though I grow older I do not grow wiser—I could think of numerous different outcomes for this film. These diverse solutions would all have been compromises that would have delayed death and allowed the lovers to remain together a while longer. But all these alternate endings are little but a weary recognition of the uncompromising march of time. What would have happened to *Elvira Madigan*'s idealized lovers had they stayed together? Could their love have been sustained at that very high pitch? Would it not have ended in compromises? How to retain those unique moments in which we step, whether through love, religion, or art, out of history, freeze time, loose ourselves in a timeless moment? Robert Browning's wicked poem "Porphyria's Lover" tells us of reaching this very high pitch of emotion and then at that very exquisite moment the lover, wrapping Porphyria's lovely long tresses around her neck, strangles her to death, for it was a moment that could never be recaptured. In *Time Regained* (*Le temps retrouvé*), the concluding volume of Proust's great opus, the author yearns to recapture time. For us, however, time is the enemy and its passing, a fact so imbricated in historical processes, is the ultimate fatal blow that inexorably leads to our own individual demise and to the rise and collapse of civilizations. The artist or scholar therefore wishes to stop time. The ending of *Elvira Madigan* and Browning's poem argue that the last answer may be in death that captures the swift passing of eternity and prevents, radical as this may seem, change.

One may, of course, go on indefinitely providing literary and other aesthetic examples of ways in which individuals have attempted to escape history or freeze time through their work. Although not every artist produces art in response to the terror of history, nor does every aspect of any artist's body of work focus solely on these type of responses, it may be fitting to conclude this chapter with brief notes on three nineteenth-century poets who, at least in some of their work, aim for those ephemeral but transcendental moments when time stops. All three died young and in somewhat tragic circumstances. All three led difficult lives. All three were deeply and uncompromisingly committed to their artistic vision, so that their choices, personal and artistic, deeply impacted their lives. Their lives and the burning passion of their poetical vision provide us with a road map to those aesthetic escapes from history and time.

John Keats (1795–1821), Charles Baudelaire (1821–1867), and Arthur Rimbaud (1854–1891), poets who wrote passionately early in their respective lives and died young before they grew old, tired, and cynical, tried to capture the immediacy of the moment, the sensation of ephemeral beauty. They sought, through their poetry, to hold fast to beauty against the tide of time and history. Rimbaud stopped writing at twenty-one. Keats, always afraid of the inadequacies of his poetry, burned with agony, not unlike his " knight-at-arms, alone and palely loitering" in his "La Belle Dame sans Merci." Baudelaire and, above all, his collection of poems *Les fleurs du mal*, were condemned by the French government for indecency and attacks on public morals. Rimbaud was accused of being a libertine. He lived as intensely as he wrote. For him, eternity was contained in the moment:

> Elle est retrouvée,
> Quoi? ———L'Éternité
> C'est la mer allée
> Avec le soleil.
> From *L'Éternité* (1872)

> It is found again.
> What? ———Eternity.
> It is the sea
> Fled away with the sun.
> Oliver Bernard, trans. (Arthur Rimbaud,
> *Collected Poems*, 1962)

Eternity is to be found, captured as it were, in the sunset, in the single dying of one day. Eternity, the contrary of time, is then articulated in one single moment. Time suspended, beauty, natural and poetical, encompassing and banishing time.

In Keats' "Endymion," the beautiful brings "joy for ever," granting a kind of immortality. The eponymous hero of the poem embarks in a long journey through history and time. Love and sorrow are his companions, and the poem ends in an epiphany beyond history and time. These are the same ideas about the eternity of beauty that are so powerfully articulated in his "Ode on a Grecian Urn." In the latter, the classical beauty of the urn, "… silent form, does tease us out of thought / as does eternity." All one needs to know is that "beauty is truth, truth beauty." Most of Keats' greatest poems were, of course, attempts to recover and explain what the poet saw as the timelessness beauty of classical Greek antiquity; yet, his very last poem, written in Rome as he awaited death in 1819, was dedicated to his lover, Fanny Brawne. "Bright Star," as beautiful a poem as Keats ever wrote (and turned by Jane Campion into a most lyrical film with the same title), the classical Greek urn is replaced by the memory of Fanny's "ripening breast." The poet, as he faces inexorable death, wishes only "to feel *for ever* in a sweet unrest, / Still, still to hear her tender-taken breath, / And so live *ever*—or else swoon to death [italics are mine]." And die he did shortly after finishing the poem.

Baudelaire's extraordinarily beautiful "L'invitation au voyage," his final evocation of Venice (think of the connection that Proust also had with Venice) evokes a world asleep, in which the beauty and colors of the city, lit by a radiant sun, puts nature and time itself into deep slumber. What remains is an eternal world, lived as in the case of Rimbaud in the intensity of the day, of beauty, luxury, calm, and voluptuousness:

> *Les soleils couchants*
> *Revêtent les champs,*
> *Les canaux, la ville entière,*
> *D'hyacinthe et d'or;*
> *Le monde s'endort*
> *Dans une chaude lumière.*
> *Là, tout n'est qu'ordre et beauté,*
> *Luxe, calme et volupté.*
>   From *Les Fleurs du Mal* (1857)

> The sun, going down,
> With its glory will crown
> The canals, the whole city,
> With hyacinth and gold;
> The world falls asleep
> In a warm glow of light.
> There all is order and beauty,
> Luxury, peace, and pleasure.
>   William Aggeler, trans. (*The Flowers*
>   *of Evil*, 1954)

The world, history, and time, of course, did not sleep. It did not slumber, as did John of the Cross' soul in his *Dark Night of the Soul,* upon the beloved "flowery breast." Four years after Baudelaire's death of cancer at the age of forty-six, the Prussian armies marched into Paris. The *communards,* opposing the invaders and the French bourgeois government that had so supinely surrendered, were massacred at the butte of Montmartre, hunted down and executed throughout Paris by provincial French militias.

CONCLUSION

IF I CONCLUDED THE PREVIOUS CHAPTER with a brief review of three nineteenth century poets, it was because poetry, bound at one and the same time by fixed rules and artifice and by the creative spirit, may also break through, by the sheer beauty and power of words, to the very heart of things. The Greeks thought of poetry as coming from the gods, an effortless and spontaneous journey into the beautiful. Poets, especially nineteenth-century poets, followed strict notions of rhyme, meter, and rhythm. Yet, as we saw in Keats, Baudelaire, and Rimbaud's work, these poets allowed their vision to transcend the rigid structures of the poetic composition. They sought to escape both the constraints of history and poetical structures by timeless grace. It was not so with all poets. James Thomson (1834–1882), whose life overlapped those of Baudelaire and Rimbaud, wrote not of redemption or escape but of his dark vision of his world—London specifically—as he saw it. In his "The City of Dreadful Night," some of the stanzas are as pessimistic as any one could find in Western literature. Thomson has not too many fans nowadays, but I remember reading these verses in the mid 1960s and feeling as if I had discovered some kindred pessimistic soul. Here they are, these sad words:

> And now at last authentic word I bring,
> Witnessed by every dead and living thing;
> Good tidings of great joy for you, for all:

There is no God; no Fiend with names divine
Made us and tortures us; if we must pine,
It is to satiate no Being's gall.

It was the dark delusion of a dream,
That living Person conscious and supreme,
Whom we must curse for cursing us with life;
Whom we must curse because the life he gave
Could not be buried in the quiet grave,
Could not be killed by poison or the knife.

This little life is all we must endure,
The grave's most holy peace is ever sure,
We fall asleep and never wake again;
Nothing is of us but the mouldering flesh,
Whose elements dissolve and merge afresh
In earth, air, water, plants, and other men.
James Thomson (1874)

I apologize for concluding with so dark a vision. I have already, to be sure, warned the reader that neither my reflections on these matters nor even the accumulated experience of all my years bring either wisdom or solace. In truth, I am as clueless about the world in my advanced years as I was early in life. I wish desperately, here and in my life, to come to some conclusion that in the clarity of its formulation would provide a convincing answer as to how to confront and live with history's terror and the passing of time. I dismissed self-help books in my introduction, and this is certainly not one. I have spent most of my life on a journey in search of meaning. I sought first to make sense of the world— and of myself in the world—through religion. I either failed or reached a point at which religious answers sounded empty and meaningless to me. I know that these answers, though they may be comforting for others, are not for me. Once again, I do not wish to convince anyone that his or her religious beliefs are false. I have my own problems to worry about, but, with Thomson, I assert there is no god.

I tried other avenues. Never have I embraced a life entirely of the senses, but I may have some envious thoughts as to the possibility of such a life. The way I was conditioned early on as an adolescent by certain types of readings has always prevented me from acting fully along the lines of sensory rejections of history and time. I have loved. I do love. I love my work and teaching. I read voraciously. I make meaning constantly and raise the meaning that I construct so earnestly and laboriously as a buttress against the cold, to cite Camus once again, indifference of the universe. As to seeking a refuge in aesthetic productions, I cannot write poetry (as much as I have always wanted to). I cannot paint. I cannot sing. I write monographic research books that are read by four people. Three of them are my friends and agree with everything I say. The other is usually an enemy who thinks it is all wrong.

In some of my classes, discussing Greek philosophy, I tell the students, half-humorously, that after the demise of the great and comprehensive philosophical systems of Plato and, far more so, Aristotle, the world that followed embraced peculiar philosophical ideas centered on man. Tracing the transformation of the Greek world after Alexander and the rise of Hellenism, I describe the emergence of Stoicism, Epicureanism, and Skepticism. Tongue in cheek, I try to explain this in somewhat theatrical fashion. I tell them that Stoics accepted pain unflinchingly, pursued ethical forms of life, found meaning in the face of a cruel and distant universe and the absence of gods. I describe my continuous preaching in the classroom about values, about doing the right thing, about choosing to do the good as a form of "public" reaffirmation of Stoic ideals. And then, I go home. I pour myself a glass of wine (always red of course). I read novels. I put my feet up. Epicureans sought to avoid pain, to find in moderation and friendship the route to happiness. Everything strongly felt led eventually to misery.

And then my wife disturbs my calm and reminds me of the garbage pail that has to be emptied and thrown out in the garbage dump. Reluctantly and not very happily, I try to delay, I resist doing the chore. Eventually I go to the bathroom to take a shower. I am alone. I look at myself in the mirror. I see nothingness around and in front of me. Nothing is to be accepted. Nothing is to be believed. I tell my students that all of us are Stoics in public, Epicureans at home, and, in the depths of our hearts, Skeptics. As cynical and humorously intended as this is, there is some great element of truth in it. We are many things at the same time. The Stoic in us overlaps with the Epicurean and the Skeptic. I think that as futile as the struggle against history and time is, one must endure. One must continue to make meaning, howsoever one seeks to make meaning. We need to keep pushing the wheel. The world has beauty in it. It comes in many forms. It is all around us. It makes the horror, if not worthwhile, at least somewhat bearable. I am not betraying my often-dark vision and pessimistic outlook by writing this. My skepticism remains. But one must also acknowledge that we live because of those moments of beauty, of pleasure, of meaning that allow us to keep on going.

One of my favorite stories is by Julio Cortázar, an Argentinean writer. It is a short story entitled "The Yellow Flower." In the story, Cortázar tells us of a man who lives in Paris. He sees a young boy who replicates himself at that age. He is horrified by the awareness and sudden knowledge that his miserable and tedious life is going to be repeated *ad infini-*

tum, that we are caught in some endless cycle of existence in which we are condemned never to rest but to repeat our sufferings and mistakes again and again. He insinuates himself into the boy's family. He becomes a friend, and then he kills the boy. His first reaction is one of exaltation for having stopped the cycle of existence, for not having to do this again. But on his way out of the scene of his crime, he sees a beautiful yellow flower. He is now swept by regret for having deprived the young boy of the opportunity to see that yellow flower in some far-away future. I have seen a yellow flower. All my complaints and pessimism are nothing compared to the single awareness of that yellow flower and of the beautiful. Sometimes I complain to my mother of my aches, of the indignities of growing old. Her answer is always the same: "Think of the alternative," she says. The alternative is death. The alternative is worse. Yet Tolkien, in a luminous aside in his *Silmarillion*, reminds us that the great gift of the Valars (the gods of his magical world) to humans was death. And when death comes, as it will, for time will not spare us, then, at least, we can keep doing some good. We return to the earth.

The escape from and the struggle against history is, after all, an escape from and a struggle against time. Since we are not coming back at all, regardless of what religion may say, and since, while we now may prolong life though at a price, the only way we can conquer time is through work and deeds that propel us into a future that we, ourselves, will never experience. The option is to cheat time and history by exiting as soon as possible or, at least, to escape completely at those moments in which ephemerally we seem to step out of history altogether. In the end, the roads followed by aesthetes and scholars only provide one more option, one more means for facing down the terror of history. Or as Thomson puts it:

The grave's most holy peace is ever sure,
We fall asleep and never wake again;
Nothing is of us but the mouldering flesh,
Whose elements dissolve and merge afresh
In earth, air, water, plants, and other men.
　　"The City of Dreadful Night"

We survive, against time and history, in memory, in earth, air, water, plants, and other men. In the end, Goya's horrific and powerful painting, *Saturn Eating His Children*, portrays something that both the ancient Greeks and the Mexica in the valley of Mexico knew very well. Time will eat all of us, but that is really fine. It is as it should be. Or as an ancient Nahua poem expressed it:

We live HERE on the earth [stamping on the mud floor]
we are all fruits of the earth
the earth sustains us
we grow here, on the earth and flower
and when we die we wither in the earth
we are ALL FRUITS of the earth [stamping on the mud floor].
We eat of the earth
then the earth eats us.[1]

[1] As cited in Inga Clendinnen, *Aztecs* (Cambridge: Cambridge University Press, 1991) 263.

INDEX

religion: author's experience, 35–36, 48, 68–69, 77–81; belief *vs.* knowledge, 39–40; morality argument, 44; and mysticism, 27–28; and political power, 40–44, 61–62, 70, 74–77
religion as escape: ancient world, 57–58, 60, 91; category boundary challenges, 85–87; Christianity's role, 57–59; fear's role, 64–66; Katrina example, xiv; and material world embracement, 85–86, 91–92; millennial movements, 28–29, 54–55, 62–64, 72–77; overview, 17–19, 27–29, 36, 44–48, 56–57; plague example, xii–xiii; rapture expectations, 38–39, 60–61; resistance element, 55–56, 61–62, 72–77; role of Francis of Assisi, 48–55; tradition of, 59–60; witch craze, 29, 46, 65–72; wrathful god explanation, 36–38, 71–72
Religious Warfare (Housley), 18–19
Remedies of Love (Ovid), 117
Republic (Plato), 44, 125, 144–45, 147, 153
resistance: and religion, 55–56, 61–62, 72–77; and sexual pleasure, 123
Restif de la Bretonne, 122–23
Rimbaud, Arthur, 163–64
Rome, 57–59, 94–95
routines, daily, xiii–xiv, 90, 98–102, 150–52, 158–59
Ruskin, John, 153
Russell, Jeffrey Burton, 56

Sabbatai Zevi, 62–63
Santa Barbara story, 108–16
Santería ceremony, 68–69
Santillana, 24
Saturn Eating His Children (Goya), 25, 172

Satyricon (Petronius), 94–95
scholarly life, Huxley's appraisal, 129–31. *See also* writing response
Schwartz-Bart, André, 134
science fiction/fantasy, 31, 147–48, 171
Scientific Revolution, unreason parallels, 9
Sebastianism, 34, 73
security, unpredictability, 13
sensual pleasure. *See* material world, embracement as escape
Sentimental Education (Flaubert), 112
September 11 attacks, 13, 61
sexual pleasure as escape, 92–94, 120–27, 130. *See also* love
Shakers, 126
short stories, author's, 107–16, 135–36
Silmarillion (Tolkien), 171
Smith, Winston, 100, 123
Solon, 22
Sophocles, 14–15, 26, 160
Spain, 34, 73
Sparta, 145
Stoicism, 169–70
The Stranger (Camus), 6, 26, 160
Strayer, Joseph R., 90
El sueño de la razón produce monstruos (Goya), 6, 7f
suicide, 118–19, 149, 150
Swann's Way (Proust), 155–56
Sybaris, 92
Symposium (Plato), 117

Tacitus, 94–95
technological advances, unreason parallels, 9–11, 46–47
terror/anxiety of history, overview: escape strategies summarized, 15–22, 25–34; as reality, 4–9, 150–52, 171–72; writing challenges, 10–17, 23–25. *See also* aesthetics